exploring HEAVENLY PLACES

Revealing of the sons of God

VOLUME 2

PAUL L. COX
ROB GROSS

EXPLORING HEAVENLY PLACES
Revealing of the sons of God
Volume 2

Paul L. Cox and Rob Gross

Aslan's Place Publications
9315 Sagebrush
Apple Valley, CA 92308
760-810-0990

aslansplace.com

Unless otherwise noted, all scripture quotations are from the New King James Version of the Bible. Copyright © 1979, 1980, 1982 by Thomas Nelson, Inc., publishers. Used by permission. Scripture quotations marked KJV are from the King James Version of the Bible.

Scripture quotations marked NIV are from the Holy Bible, New International Version. Copyright © 1973, 1978, 1984, 2010, 2011, International Bible Society. Used by permission.

Scripture quotations marked YOUNG'S are from Young's Literal Translations by Robert Young, 1989. Reprinted by Baker Book House, Grand Rapids, Michigan, copyright © 2003.

Greek definitions are derived from Strong's Greek Concordance.
Hebrew definitions are derived from Strong's Hebrew Concordance.

Copyright 2014 by Paul Cox and Rob Gross
All rights reserved.
Cover design and layout by Brodie Schmidtke
ISBN # 979-8-55334-386-6
Printed in the United States of America

TABLE OF CONTENTS

Introduction 4

Chapter 1: *The Dream* 5-8

Chapter 2: *Rethinking Conception* 9-11

Chapter 3: *Who Are the sons of God?* 12-14

Chapter 4: *Sons of God, or Angels?* 15-16

Chapter 5: *Identifying the sons of God* 17-20

Chapter 6: *The Ultimate Conspiracy* 21-25

Chapter 7: *The Fallen sons of God* 26-29

Chapter 8: *Moloch and the Fallen sons of God* 30-33

Chapter 9: *Israel and the Fallen sons of God* 34-41

Chapter 10: *Generational Relevance of the Fallen sons in Israel* 42-46

Chapter 11: *Generational Relevance of the sons of God Today* 47-50

Chapter 12: *The Revealed sons of God* 51-56

Chapter 13: *The Foundational Gate* 57-59

Chapter 14: *The Orphan Stronghold* 60-66

Chapter 15: *Melchizedek and the Gift of Discernment* 67-72

Chapter 16: *Melchizedek's War* 73-74

Chapter 17: *Prayer of Restitution* 75-82

Chapter 18: *Ruling and Reigning With Christ* 83-86

Chapter 19: *Introduction to the Prayer to Establish Us as Kings and Priests* .. 87-88

Chapter 20: *Prayer to Establish Us as Kings and Priests in His Kingdom* 89-92

Appendix 93-113

Glossary 114-128

Introduction

Exploring Heavenly Places, Volume 2 is a collaborative effort of Paul L Cox and Rob Gross, which delves into the revelation they have received and the research they have done regarding the true identities of such ancient entities as Moloch and Baal, the fallen sons of God, Lucifer, Satan, the Nephilim and Rephaim, and the revealed sons of God.

In general, Paul's contributions deal mostly with the revelation, giving a clear picture of how God began and continues to show us about these issues. He also shares real-life examples of how people's lives today are still affected by the events of Biblical history.

Rob's contribution is a systematic study that begins in Genesis and encompasses scriptures throughout the Bible to provide an accurate historical picture that illustrates the lasting spiritual ramifications that have resonated down through the years.

Also included are three generational prayers that were developed in group settings to deal with the fallout of our ancestors' sins in our lives and an appendix that offers many of the exact prophetic words that have been received.

We sincerely hope that *Exploring Heavenly Places, Volume 2* will be as exciting to you as it is to us, and pray that the Lord will grant wisdom and understanding to each reader.

CHAPTER ONE

The Dream

It was just another dream, or so I thought. In the midst of my first ministry trip to Hong Kong in August 2011, I woke up abruptly, remembering a vivid dream of a man chasing me through the aisles of a supermarket. He said, "I am a senator and I have a right to chase you because of Acts 7." Suddenly the scene changed and I was crawling through a chain link fence, and then found myself riding a bicycle. I must have been very good at it because I was hands-free on the bike, holding my droid phone, and watching the Star Wars movie all at the same time. I became somewhat frustrated as I attempted to delete the movie off of my phone and couldn't. I turned to my right and said to a man walking beside me, "I want to delete Stars Wars off on my phone." His response was not helpful! "It is not possible," he replied.

As I lay in bed pondering the dream, my first thought was that there is nothing about stars in Acts 7, but I grabbed a Bible and looked it up anyway. To say I was stunned would be to minimize the impact those verses had on me. The dream felt like the experience early explorers must have had when they came over a ridge and discovered a new land. Yet even with the excitement of my initial discovery, the overview eventually faded away and became the settling and taking of a spiritual land—a land that has proven to be the location of many buried treasures. These mined treasures have been refined by the Holy Spirit to produce mighty works of God; and now there seems to be no end to the surprises.

Together we will survey the land, and do not be surprised if the Lord brings deeper levels of spiritual and physical healing to you. Do not be surprised if you find evangelism easier; do not be surprised if a time of being disconnected with the Lord begins to fade as you surrender to an intimacy with God such as you've never dreamed possible.

Our journey began with a familiar passage in Acts 7. Having preached though the book of Acts, I knew the material well; so how could I have missed what was really written there? I had to admit that I had totally misunderstood the message.

Acts 7 is a sermon by Stephen; delivered to the Jews who doubted the resurrection of Jesus. It is perhaps the best biblical summary of the Old Testament. Scanning the chapter and trying to find some mention of stars, my eyes fell on verse 43:

> *You also took up the tabernacle of Moloch, and the star of your god Remphan[1], images which you made to worship; and I will carry you away beyond Babylon.*

There it was! Stars are actually mentioned in Acts 7, but I had to dig deeper. Stephen was quoting from the Septuagint translation of Amos 5:26:

> *You also carried Sikkuth your king, and Chiun[2], your idols, the star of your gods, Which you made for yourselves.*

Rephan is the Assyrian god of Saturn, or perhaps refers to the Egyptian Sat-urn god Repa; Sikkuth is a Babylonian reference to star god Saturn[3]; and Chiun is also tied to Saturn[4], so the emphasis here seems to be on star worship. The Theological Workbook of the Old Testament makes this observation:

> It is clear from Mesopotamian myths that the stars represented the pantheon of gods [the cuneiform sign for Ishtar, the queen of heav-en (Jer 7:18, etc.) was a star]. Thus to become a vassal of Assyria and later, of Babylon, meant to serve the 'host of heaven' as gods. This is made clear in the accounts of Manasseh (II Kgs 21:3, 5) who wor-shiped these deities as a part of his subservience, and Josiah, who repudiated them as a part of his revolt against such subservience (II Kgs 23:4–5).[5]

It becomes obvious in these two passages that Moloch and Saturn are closely tied together.

About a week after the Star Wars dream, I had another dream. In this one I was watching Star Wars on my Samsung Galaxy pad, and once again trying to delete the movie. Yet it seemed the Lord was speaking to me, "Do not avoid the concept of Star Wars!" The word 'galaxy' seemed to reinforce the concept of stars, but many months passed before I thought, "What does Samsung mean?" Once again I was shocked, for an Internet search for Samsung revealed that this Korean word means three stars, with the 'three' representing something 'big, numerous and powerful'; and 'stars' meaning eternity.[6] But apparently the Lord was not finished emphasizing that I must pay attention to what is happening with the stars because I had yet another dream. In this one my son, Brian, was driving me to the Los Angeles Griffith Park Planetarium but I was very upset about going and was trying to get out of the car.

During my years of pastoring I had heard about Moloch.[7] I was also familiar with the golden idol that the children of Israel formed under the leadership of Aaron, but had not realized that the god they were worshipping was Moloch.[8] Moloch's name means king[9] and this Ammonite god was worshiped by sacrificing children.

> Its image was a hollow brazen figure, with the head of an ox, and outstretched human arms. It was heated red hot by a fire from with-in, and the little ones placed in its arms to be slowly burned, while to prevent the parents from hearing the dying cries, the sacrificing priests beat drums.[10]

Meditating on all this information I had a chain reaction of thoughts and realized I had never really understood what actually happened while Moses was on Mt. Sinai receiving the law from the Lord. While Aaron, as the High Priest of the Living God, was at the foot of the mountain entering into an ungodly blood covenant with the enemy; Yahweh was entering into an everlasting covenant with Israel on the top of the mountain. This was not merely an occasion of bowing down to another god. The people of God were offering their own children as blood sacrifices to a pagan god,[11] thus sealing a covenant that declared that Moloch was their king and not the Lord God. The resulting response from God was, "I will carry you away beyond Babylon."[12] Before the Children of Israel even entered the Promised Land, they had already been predestined to be carried off into exile.

The significance of these insights was yet to be understood, and the rabbit trail was about to lead to more unexpected territory. An investigation of Moloch revealed many scriptures that spoke of the abomination of the worship of this god. My research led me to Jeremiah 32:34–35:

> But they set their abominations in the house which is called by My name, to defile it. And they built the high places of Baal which are in the Valley of the Son of Hinnom, to cause their sons and their daughters to pass through the fire to
> Moloch, which I did not command them, nor did it come into My mind that they should do this abomination, to cause Judah to sin.

Jeremiah was establishing a clear connection between Moloch and Baal. The name 'Baal' is a Semitic noun meaning 'lord or owner', occurring about 90 times in the Old Testament and referring to a Canaanite god.[13]

He is referred to as the 'mightiest of the heroes', 'the powerful excellent one', 'the lord over the fertile land', and 'the son of EL'.[14] The belief was that Baal owned the property of those who worshiped him.[15] Baal is also connected with the underworld and considered to be the leader of the Rephaim. He is said to activate the deceased and thus played a major role in the ancestor cult. It was declared that he was lord of the great gods and of the deified ancestors.

It is clear from Scripture that the Lord God is at war with Moloch and Baal. Those who are in rebellion must forsake these gods and make Yahweh their only God.[16]

> "And it shall be, in that day," says the Lord, "That you will call Me 'My Husband,' and no longer call Me 'My Master,' for I will take from her mouth the names of the Baals, and they shall be remembered by their name no more.
> In that day I will make a covenant for them with the beasts of the field, with the birds of the air, and with the creeping things of the ground. Bow and sword of battle I will shatter from the earth, to make them lie down safely. I will betroth you to Me forever; yes, I will betroth you to Me In righteousness and justice, In loving kindness and mercy; I will betroth you to Me in faithfulness, and you shall know the Lord."

This revelation was intriguing but what did Moloch, Baal, and Saturn have to do with star wars and who was this senator in my dream?

CHAPTER TWO

Rethinking Conception

A client arrived at our ministry center to receive prayer. Nothing unusual. However, the unexpected happened. After the usual introductions, the ministry session began and I found myself posing the typical queries; that is, until a thought came into my mind that I articulated as a question before I even processed what I was actually thinking. The client never hesitated but quickly responded to the question and immediately had an open vision. Meanwhile, I pondered, "Did I really believe what I was asking?"

My question, "Ask the Lord to take you back before conception when you were a created spirit at His throne. How do you feel there?"

She saw herself before a columned raised throne. She was filled with delight.

"Ask the Lord if you wanted to come to earth." With no hesitation, "I did not want to come." "Were you willing to come to earth?"

There was silence, and then with saddened eyes she responded, "Yes, I was willing to come."

I contemplated my next question. "Did anything happen to you between leaving God's throne and coming to earth?"

She was startled. "As I am moving down the steps in front of the throne there is a wolf on my left hand side. The wolf is attacking me!"

As she was responding to my questions, I was discerning what was happening spiritually. I was aware of spiritual beings called stars. These stars, however, were not righteous but unrighteous. After the comment about the wolf, I was uncertain how to proceed. Wondering if there was some connection between a wolf and stars, I opened my laptop and typed 'wolf ' and 'stars' into the search engine. The phrase 'lupus[17] constellation' appeared on my screen. As I shared the discovery with her, she appeared stunned.

"That is why I came in for ministry today. I have Lupus."

Following the lead of the Holy Spirit we asked the Lord to break all the generational consequences of sins that had given the enemy a right to attack her physically. We asked the Lord to disconnect her from all ungodly stars, star systems, constellations and zodiacs. We concluded with prayers and shared our farewells.

During the following weeks I thought often about what had happened in that prayer session. It certainly seemed that the Lord had given us a key. I reflected on my star wars dream and wondered if the Lord was revealing a connection to me. Some months later, a client came in for ministry, sat down and began to speak.

"You don't remember me, do you?" Perplexed I replied, "No."

"I am the first person you asked the Lord to take back to His throne before conception. I am the one who had Lupus."

"Please tell me what happened."

"I went to the doctor and he performed a test. The Lupus is in remission. There is no evidence of the disease."

I was unprepared for this. She was actually healed. Has God given us a clue to the underpinnings of disease?

Over the course of several months I have asked dozens of people the same questions about their experience before conception, and have been amazed at the numbers who are aware of what it was like before they came to earth. Their stories are often similar. They see themselves as orbs of light somewhere around the throne. They speak of unspeakable joy and delight to be with their Heavenly Father. Most relate that they did not want to come to earth but were willing to come. Also common is their understanding of conflict with the enemy between leaving His throne and coming to earth. Often the conflict is violent, resulting in surprising consequences.

Is it possible that our spirits did exist before conception? I had never been willing to entertain that idea. One scripture however, Jeremiah 1:5, was troubling to me and I now found I could not avoid what it obviously declared— we were known before conception.

Before I formed you in the womb I knew you; before you were born I sanctified you; I ordained you a prophet to the nations.[18]

The Hebrew word 'knew' is 'yada', and relates here to God's knowledge of man. We were fully known before conception. I had been very comfortable believing that this verse actually meant that God knew 'about us' before conception, only in the sense that He knew whom we would become. Now it was time to rethink my interpretation. Perhaps we were known because we were actually present with him as created spirits.

I have asked easily hundreds of people what they knew about their time before conception, carefully crafting my questions and being cautious not to lead them to an answer I wanted. A vast majority has given me the similar answers. Many have told me that they have known this since childhood, but were afraid to express what they knew because of the possibility of being theologically challenged. Another one of my presumptions was falling apart. It would prove not to be the last one, for I was shocked to find out who we were and who we are.

CHAPTER THREE

Who are the sons of God?

The day after Pentecost 2010, I left for a ministry trip to the East coast. I was working with a very spiritually gifted client who would give me prophetic direction as I ministered to her. As we were praying together, the Lord seemed to be showing her a recording of an event that happened in heaven before the Garden of Eden. It was a disturbing event that involved a group of beings called the 'sons of God'. As she was viewing this scene tears came to her eyes, "There is a group of the sons of God that have rebelled against the Lord. They want to set up their own multi-universe worlds." My mind quickly did a search of Biblical references and the passage that first caught my attention was the pre-flood account of Genesis 6:1-5:

> *Now it came to pass, when men began to multiply on the face of the earth, and daughters were born to them, that the sons of God saw the daughters of men, that they were beautiful; and they took wives for themselves of all whom they chose. And the Lord said, "My Spirit shall not strive with man forever, for he is indeed flesh; yet his days shall be one hundred and twenty years." There were giants on the earth in those days, and also afterward, when the sons of God came in to the daughters of men and they bore children to them. Those were the mighty men who were of old, men of renown. Then the Lord saw that the wickedness of man was great in the earth, and that every intent of the thoughts of his heart was only evil continually.*

Is it possible there was a rebellion against God before Adam and Eve? Who are these sons of God?

The phrase 'sons of God' is bene [ha] elohim. These spiritual beings mated with the daughters of men and had children that were giants[19]. The Hebrew word is transliterated as Nephilim, and is interpreted as giants in the NKJV. The sons of God are also mentioned in Job 1 and 2 where it seems the emphasis is first on the sons of God and then on Satan [adversary].

> Now there was a day when the sons of God came to present themselves before the Lord, and Satan also came among them. And the Lord said to Satan, "From where do you come?" So Satan answered the Lord and said, "From going to and fro on the earth, and from walking back and forth on it."[20]
> Again there was a day when the sons of God came to present themselves before the Lord, and Satan came also among them to present himself before the Lord. And the Lord said to Satan, "From where do you come?" Satan answered the Lord and said, "From going to and fro on the earth, and from walking back and forth on it."[21]

Later in Job, we are told that at creation the sons of God and spiritual beings called stars rejoiced.

> Where were you when I laid the foundations of the earth? Tell Me, if you have understanding. Who determined its measurements? Surely you know! Or who stretched the line upon it? To what were its foundations fastened? Or who laid its cornerstone, When the morning stars sang together, And all the sons of God shouted for joy?[22]

It seems probable that these sons of God were tied to land areas of the earth. Notice Deuteronomy 32:7-8.

> Remember the days of old, Consider the years of many generations. Ask your father, and he will show you; your elders, and they will tell you: when the Most High divided their inheritance to the nations, when He separated the sons of Adam, He set the boundaries of the peoples according to the number of the children of Israel.

Michael Heiser maintains that it is best to translate the phrase 'children of Israel' as 'sons of God' (as mentioned in the margin of the NKJV).[23]

As I read these scriptures ideas began to come into my mind. Was there an ultimate conspiracy theory that was true?

I enjoy watching television and movies and there seems to be a common theme in many programs—the bad person is finally cornered and then declares, "This is bigger than you think. You do not know whom you are dealing with. I am only the front person for a very evil group." So I considered the possibility that the original rebellion in heaven was by the sons of God. If this was true, perhaps in order to fulfill their scheme to take over the multi-universe worlds they needed to enlist Satan as he was given authority over the earth.

I then considered Psalm 82. Let's look at these verses and make some observations.

> *God stands in the congregation of the mighty; He judges among the gods. How long will you judge unjustly, and show partiality to the wicked? Selah. Defend the poor and fatherless; Do justice to the afflicted and needy. Deliver the poor and needy; free them from the hand of the wicked. They do not know, nor do they understand; walk about in darkness; all the foundations of the earth are unstable. I said, "You are gods, and all of you are children of the Most High. But you shall die like men, and fall like one of the princes." Arise, O God, judge the earth; for You shall inherit all nations.*

God (Elohim) stands in the congregation of the mighty; the 'congregation of the mighty' being a phrase used in Genesis to describe the Nephilim.

He judges among the gods (plural), refers to the elohim. The Elohim declares to them that they are 'gods,' or 'elohim.'

All of you (plural), are children of the Most High but you will die like men perhaps speaks of the Nephilim who died. It would seem that these fallen sons of God did evil and their wickedness would be punished.

One of the issues that must be discussed is the term 'sons of God'.

CHAPTER FOUR

Sons of God, or Angels?

In Christian theology we have the tendency to categorize all spiritual beings under the all-encompassing heading of angels (angelology). I grew up with this understanding, and my theological training only reinforced this notion. As the Lord taught me to discern, I noticed that I feel different spiritual beings on different parts of my head and wondered if it is possible that spiritual beings are different in the spiritual world even as there are different types of beings in the physical creation. For example we do not classify all four-legged animals as dogs. Therefore, it makes sense that in the spiritual world we have beings called angels, seraphim, cherubim, elders, etc. There are not simply different kinds of angels, but are different kinds of spiritual beings. Another way of saying this would be to articulate that the Bible means what it says. In other words, when the writers of the Bible mentioned 'sons of God' they did not mean angels. But, it is at this point that we have a potential problem. In the New Testament we have two possible references to the sons of God that refer to them as angels.

> *For if God did not spare the angels who sinned, but cast them down to hell and delivered them into chains of darkness, to be reserved for judgment; and did not spare the ancient world, but saved Noah, one of eight people, a preacher of righteousness, bringing in the flood on the world of the ungodly; and turning the cities of Sodom and Gomorrah into ashes, condemned them to destruction, mak-ing them an example to those who afterward would live ungodly; and delivered righteous Lot, who was oppressed by the filthy conduct of the wicked.[24]*

15

But I want to remind you, though you once knew this, that the Lord, having saved the people out of the land of Egypt, afterward destroyed those who did not believe. And the angels who did not keep their proper domain, but left their own abode, He has reserved in everlasting chains under darkness for the judgment of the great day; as Sodom and Gomorrah, and the cities around them in a similar manner to these, having given themselves over to sexual immorality and gone after strange flesh, are set forth as an example, suffering the vengeance of eternal fire.[25]

How do we address these two passages? I have some possible solutions, understanding that what I am suggesting may be a new thought.[26]

The word 'angel' is the Greek angelos, and means messenger. This translation is used in Luke 7:27,

This is he of whom it is written: "Behold, I send My messenger [angelos] before Your face, Who will prepare Your way before You."

The term 'angel' in the two passages above from 2 Peter and Jude is tied to what happened in Sodom and Gomorrah, and not to the time before the flood.

Not only did the 'sons of God' have sexual relationships with the daughters of men, but angels did as well.

CHAPTER FIVE

Identifying the Sons of God

As I indicated before, the revelation about the sons of God was unfolding. More ideas came. Were we actually sons of God before conception? Or per-haps we are the revealed sons of God spoken of in Romans 8? Cautiously, I started presenting this idea in different coaching sessions and the response was positive. I was stunned. How could this be? Was there any scriptural support?

I was not prepared for what I was to discover. Consider first the passage in Romans 8:18-19

> *For I consider that the sufferings of this present time are not worthy to be com-pared with the glory, which shall be revealed in us. For the earnest expectation of the creation eagerly waits for the revealing of the sons of God.*

I wondered if the sons of God mentioned in the Old Testament were the same sons of God mentioned here in Romans 8, so I checked the Septuagint translation of the Hebrew bible and, indeed, it is the same phrase. Other scriptures came to light. Notice 1 Samuel 28:9–14:

> *Then the woman said to him, "Look, you know what Saul has done, how he has cut off the mediums and the spiritists from the land. Why then do you lay a snare for my life, to cause me to die?" And Saul swore to her by the L*ord*, saying, "As the L*ord *lives, no punishment shall come upon you for this thing." Then the woman said, "Whom shall I bring up for you?" And he said, "Bring up Samuel for me."*

When the woman saw Samuel, she cried out with a loud voice. And the woman spoke to Saul, saying, "Why have you deceived me? For you are Saul!" And the king said to her, "Do not be afraid. What did you see?" And the woman said to Saul, "I saw a spirit ascending out of the earth." So he said to her, "What is his form?"

And she said, "An old man is coming up, and he is covered with a mantle." And Saul perceived that it was Samuel, and he stooped with his face to the ground and bowed down.

In this historical account Saul had gone to the medium of Endor so he could talk to the deceased Samuel. The medium was successful but shocked. When Saul asked her what she saw, it is her response that is very interesting. She said, "I saw an 'elohim' coming up and his form is an old man covered with a mantle." This is a striking comment. She described what she saw as an 'elohim', and his form was that of an old man called Samuel.

In Kaneohe, Hawaii, I was sharing my thoughts about the sons of God, carefully characterizing my remarks with the question, "What if this is true?" A man came up to me and said he wanted to discuss this further. I had my defenses up and was ready for an argument, knowing that I was not really confident enough in my thoughts to argue the veracity of what I was saying. He told me to look up Luke 3:37-38, which details the supposed line of Joseph coming down to the Messiah. Luke starts with Joseph and works backwards in the generations. the son of Methuselah, the son of Enoch, the son of Jared, the son of Mahalalel, the son of Cainan, the son of Enosh, the son of Seth, the son of Adam, the son of God. Luke is very precise. Adam is a son of God.[27]

Now consider Luke 20. The Sadducees asked Jesus about a woman that marries a man with seven brothers. She marries each successively but all seven die. Who would the woman be married to in heaven? Jesus' response is recorded in Luke 20:34-36:

Jesus answered and said to them, "The sons of this age marry and are given in marriage. But those who are counted worthy to attain that age, and the resur-rection from the dead, neither marry nor are given in marriage; nor can they die anymore, for they are equal to the angels and are sons of God, being sons of the resurrection.

Jesus' made it clear that heaven is not like earth. In heaven there is no marital sex. The phrase for they are equal to the angels is a translation of the Greek word, isangeloi:

> In the New Testament the only occurrence is in Luke 20:36, which tells us that the resurrected will know neither mortality nor sexual intercourse, since they are like angels.[28]

Now look at the context. Jesus is saying that 'sons of this age' are like the angels in that they are not involved in marital sex. That is how they are like the angels. The text does not say the sons of this age are the same as angels. Jesus also declares that the sons of this age are the 'sons of God'.

In Matthew 13:36-43, Jesus explores the tension between the sons of the Kingdom and the sons of the wicked one. It is not too far a stretch to see that Jesus could be speaking about the righteous sons of God and the unrighteous sons of God.[29] The influence of the fallen sons of God of mankind will be explored later in this book.

> *Then Jesus sent the multitude away and went into the house. And His disciples came to Him, saying, "Explain to us the parable of the tares of the field." He answered and said to them: "He who sows the good seed is the Son of Man. The field is the world, the good seeds are the sons of the kingdom, but the tares are the sons of the wicked one. The enemy who sowed them is the devil, the harvest is the end of the age, and the reapers are the angels. Therefore as the tares are gathered and burned in the fire, so it will be at the end of this age. The Son of Man will send out His angels, and they will gather out of His kingdom all things that offend, and those who practice lawlessness, and will cast them into the furnace of fire. There will be wailing and gnashing of teeth. Then the righteous will shine forth as the sun in the kingdom of their Father. He who has ears to hear, let him hear!*

As I was doing research on the concept of the sons of God, I came across an article in Collins Thesaurus of the Bible. Notice how the author pulls together the concept of the children of God into the arena of the sons of God.

> *The Spirit testifies with our spirit that we are children of God (Rom. 8:16); because you are sons, God sent the Spirit of his Son (Gal. 4:6); all who are led by the Spirit of God are sons of God (Rom. 8:14); sons of God through faith in Christ Jesus (Gal. 3:26); to those who believe in his name he gave the right to become children of God (John 1:12); you shall be my sons and daughters (2 Cor. 6:18); sons of the living God (Hos. 1:10; Rom. 9:26); you will be sons of the Most High (Luke 6:35); now we are children of God (1 John 3:2); what love,*

19

that we should be called children of God (1 John 3:1); the sons of the resurrection are sons of God (bold for emphasis) (Luke 20:36); I will be his God and he will be my son (Rev. 21:7); he will see his offspring (Isa. 53:10); bringing many sons to glory (Heb. 2:10); Jesus died to gather into one the children of God scattered abroad (John 11:52); it is not the children of the flesh who are the children of God but the children of the promise (Rom. 9:8); you are no longer a slave but a son (Gal. 4:7); the exhortation addressed to you as sons (Heb. 12:5); by this we know the children of God and the children of the devil (1 John 3:10).[30]

Scripture is clear that there are other gods and these gods are called the elohim. Exodus 18:11 is one reference:

Now I know that the Lord is greater than all the gods [elohim]; for in the very thing in which they behaved proudly, He was above them. [31]

Let's summarize:

1. *There is a group of created spiritual beings called sons of God that existed in heaven.*
2. *We who are alive, and all those who have previously lived, were sons of God before conception.*
3. *Some of these sons of God rebelled against God and bypassed God's created order of coming to earth through conception and mated with the daughters of men.*
4. *These spiritual beings were seen as gods by those on earth and became the gods of the pantheons on the nations of earth, i.e. the 'gods of the peoples'.*
5. *The result of this sexual activity of these fallen sons of God was the birth of the Nephilim.*
6. *One must be redeemed by the blood of Jesus Christ. Those who are redeemed become the children of God.*
7. *All creation is waiting for those of us who are the redeemed children of God to realize that we are sons of God. All creation is waiting for the revealing of the sons of God.*
8. *Nimrod was a mighty one.*
9. *The pantheon of gods are the fallen sons of God*

CHAPTER SIX

The Ultimate Conspiracy

*Now there was a day when the sons of God came to present themselves before the L*ord*, and Satan came also among them.*[32]

Whether it's the Bermuda Triangle, the assassination of JFK, or UFO sightings, conspiracy theories have abounded throughout history. Does the verse above refer to a conspiracy theory; which, according to Wikipedia, is:

> An explanatory proposition that accuses two or more people, a group, or an organization of having caused or covered up, through deliberate collusion, an event or phenomena of great social, political or economic impact.[33]

Who are the sons of God and why did Satan walk among them? These and other questions will be answered as we examine Satan's plan to pollute the gene pool of the Messiah, and block Him from coming forth.

The Grand Announcement:

Then God said, "Let us make man in our image, according to our likeness; let them have dominion over the fish of the sea, over the birds of the air, and on the cattle, over all, the earth and creeping things that creep on earth." So God created man in his own image in the image of God he created him, male and female He created them.[34]

On the sixth day of creation God shook the heavens when He declared that

He would create mankind, not in 'His' image, but in 'our' image according to our likeness. To whom did the Lord make this startling declaration? Most scholars believe that these verses refer to the Trinity, but Psalm 82:1-8 suggests otherwise:

> God stands in the congregation of the mighty; He judges among the gods. How long will you judge unjustly and show partially to the wicked? Defend the poor and fatherless; do justice to the afflicted and needy. Deliver the poor and needy; free them from the hand of the wicked. They do not know, nor do they under-stand, they walk about in darkness; all the foundations of the earth are unstable.
>
> "I (God) said, 'You are gods and all of your children [sons] of the Most High. But you shall die like men, and fall like one of the princes.'" Arise O God, judge the earth; for you shall inherit all nations.

The Divine Council:

The New King James Version explains that God took His place before the 'congregation of the Mighty' while other translations say that He stood in the 'divine council'. What is the divine council and who are its members? What can we learn from the passage above?

The Hebrew word for 'gods' is 'elohim'. At first glance, this is confusing because the Hebrew word for 'God' is also 'Elohim'. In an article entitled, "So, What Exactly is Elohim?" Michael Heiser defines elohim as "…a being whose proper habitation is the spirit world."[35] Heiser continues:

> But why refer to spiritual beings as elohim? The association is not difficult to understand, actually. Since God is a spirit, and in fact the supreme Spirit and He is the father of all spirits,[36] then the realm of the spirits is where God lives. The beings who belong to the spirit realm are therefore divine. The best word to capture that concep-tion is 'elohim'. An elohim is a divine being, in that an elohim is an inhabitant of the spiritual plane of reality."[37]

The gods referred to in Psalm 82:1-8 are lesser elohim, in contrast to God who is the all-powerful, all knowing Elohim. Why is this important? It is important because God's 'grand announcement' that He would create mankind in 'our' image referred directly to a group of spiritual beings called 'the sons of God' in Psalm 82:6.

> I God (Elohim) said, "You are gods (elohim), and all of you are children (sons of the Most High)."

Could it be, as Paul Cox proposed earlier, that we are the sons of God? Is it possible that before conception we enjoyed our Heavenly Father's presence as elohim or the sons of God?[38]

In John 10:30-36, the Pharisees intended to stone Jesus because He claimed divinity. Jesus' response in verses 34-36 is a direct quote of Psalm 82:6:

> *"Is it not written in your law I said, 'You are gods?' If He called them gods to whom the word of God came (and the Scripture cannot be broken), do you say of Him whom the Father sanctified and sent into the world, 'You are blaspheming,' because I said, 'I am the Son of God?'"*

The Greek word for 'gods' in this passage is 'theos' which is also the Greek word for 'God'. Jesus referred to the Jewish people as the sons of God and to Himself as the Son of God – amazing! (Note the difference in capitalization—only Jesus Himself is ever identified as Son. This is also important in terms of 'god(s)' versus 'God'.)

The Fall:

> *So when the woman saw that the tree was good for food, that it was pleasant to the eyes, and a tree desirable to make one wise, she took of its fruit and ate. Then the eyes of both of them were opened, and they knew they were naked; and they sewed fig leaves together and made themselves coverings.[39]*

In Luke 3:1-38 we find the genealogy of Jesus Christ. Tracing backward, Luke lists Jesus first and ends with Adam. In Luke 3:38 He refers to Adam as the son of God. Not the Son of God, but the son of God.

Adam was the first 'revealed son of God.' God formed him out of the dust of the ground and breathed into him the breath of life and he became a living being.[40] As a revealed son of God Adam was endowed with five supernatural attributes:[41]

1. Extraordinary physical strength and stamina[42]
2. Immortality[43]
3. The ability to communicate with God face to face[44]
4. Interspecies communication[45]
5. Incredible brain capacity – Adam named all of the animals and birds[46]

Adam possessed something that Satan did not have but clearly coveted, dominion, the divinely given authority to rule and reign in the heavenly places and on the earth. [47] Because of this Satan appeared to Eve as a serpent in order to, "...invert the very design of God"[48] and steal the authority that God had imparted to her and Adam and the sons of God. As mentioned earlier, Luke 3:38 refers to Adam as the son of God, which clearly implies then that we, as Adam's descendants, are the sons of God too.[49]

Satan is Held Accountable:

Soon after the Fall, God addressed Satan and held him accountable for his actions in the garden of Eden.

> *So the Lord God said to the serpent: "Because you have done this, you are cursed more than all cattle, and more than every beast of the field; on your belly you shall go, and you shall eat dust all the days of your life. And I will put enmity between you and the woman, and between your seed and her seed; He shall bruise (crush) your head and you shall bruise (crush) His heel."[50]*

God cursed Satan and put him on notice. Restating the verse above, the parenthetical additions highlight the emphatic nature of God's words:

> *"I (God) will put enmity (hostility or hatred) between you (Satan) and the woman (Eve) and between your seed (unregenerate mankind) and her (Eve's) seed (God's people); He (a man from the line of Adam) shall bruise (crush) your (Satan's) head and you (Satan) shall bruise (crush) His heel (Jesus' feet on the cross)."*

Just when Satan thought that he had permanently severed man's relationship with God and rendered him spiritually inoperable, God changed everything and said (paraphrased), "I will raise up a man from the line of Adam who will undo what you have done. He will not only reconcile my sons (and daughters) to Me, but I will give Him the authority to re-position them in the heavenly places to rule and reign as originally intended."

The Ultimate Conspiracy:

When Satan heard that a man from Adam's line would crush his head and restore the sons of God's authority to rule and reign he set in motion an insidious plan to block His coming, and what transpired next seems like a scene from a science fiction thriller. Job 1:6 tells us that when the sons of God presented themselves before the Lord, Satan came along to convince them to rebel against God—to leave the divine council and take possession of the earth by spawning a hybrid race of giants. These half-divine, half-human beings would genetically pollute the line of Adam and wage war with his descendants so the Second Adam[51] could not come forth.

24

Far fetched as this may sound, Genesis 6:1-2,4 tells us that this is exactly what transpired:

> *Now it came to pass, when men began to multiply on the face of the earth, and daughters were born to them, that the sons of God saw the daughters of men, that they were beautiful; and they took wives for themselves of all whom they chose... There were giants on the earth in those days, and also afterward, when the sons of God came into the daughters of men and they bore children to them. Those were the mighty men who were of old, men of renown.*

CHAPTER SEVEN

The Fallen Sons of God

The Flood:

In this chapter we will refer to the sons of God as the 'fallen sons of God'. Although it is impossible to know how many giants they spawned we can say with certainty that the Nephilim contributed to an already deteriorating situation:

> *Then the Lord saw that the wickedness of man was great in the earth, and that every intent of the thoughts of his heart was only evil continually. And the Lord was sorry that He had made man on the earth, and He was grieved in His heart. So the Lord said, 'I will destroy man whom I have created from the face of the earth, both man and beast, creeping things and birds of the air, for I am sorry that I have made them.'*
> 52

We do not know when the Flood occurred but scholars generally agree that the deluge was sometime between 3,600 and 3,000 B.C.[53] God's intent at this point was to 'reboot' the system and start over. According to Genesis 6:4, the giants survived the Flood, indicating that they possessed superhuman strength and great height.

Noah's Family Tree:

Although God destroyed humanity, Noah found favor with the Lord.[54] His three sons Shem, Ham and Japheth and their wives were chosen by God to repopulate the earth.[55]

To further embrace the revelation of the fallen sons of God we need to examine how they infiltrated the generational line of Adam. Luke 3:23-38 lists the genealogy of Jesus, in which Noah is listed at the tenth generation after Adam. [56] Genesis 9:1 tells us that God blessed Noah and his sons and said to them, "Be fruitful and multiply and fill the earth." Meanwhile, the fallen sons of God who had survived the Flood continued to defile the gene pool of humanity.

Noah Curses Canaan:

Genesis 9:18-27 reveals that Noah was sexually defiled by his son, Ham, indicating that Satan's plan was succeeding:

Now the sons of Noah who went out of the ark were Shem, Ham, and Japheth, and Ham was the father of Canaan. These three were the sons of Noah, and from these the whole earth was populated.

And Noah began to be a farmer, and he planted a vineyard. Then he drank of the wine and was drunk, and became uncovered in his tent. And Ham, the father of Canaan, saw the nakedness of his father, and told his two brothers outside. But Shem and Japheth took a garment, laid it on both their shoulders, and went backward and covered the nakedness of their father. Their faces were turned away, and they did not see their father's nakedness.

So Noah awoke from his wine, and knew what his younger son had done to him. Then he said: "Cursed be Canaan; a servant of servants He shall be to his brethren."

Scripture doesn't indicate what Ham did to his father. Some suggest that he sexually molested Noah while others contend that he merely gazed upon his naked body. Whatever Ham's sin was against Noah it was severe enough that his father cursed his son Canaan. Centuries later, the 'Canaanites' became a constant snare for God's people because of their rampant sexual practices.[57]

Because of these sexually immoral practices, the Canaanites were entrapped in the ungodly length, which is a spiritual place within the heavenly realms where the orphan spirit resides. It is a barren, lonely place where the sexually immoral live disconnected from the Father.[58]

The Promise:

Ten generations after Noah God quietly prompted a Chaldean named Abram to leave his father's household and go to a land far away that he did not know.[59] Trusting God, Abram packed his belongings and set out by faith with his wife, Sarai, and his nephew, Lot. Satan did not know that God was about to trans-form Abram from a moon worshipper into the father of many nations and that from his descendants the Messiah would arise to 'bruise' his head as God had earlier declared.[60]

The Nations' Inheritance:

God's call on Abram was clear: through him all the families of the earth—the nations—would be blessed! Prior to Abram's call the Lord scattered seventy nations throughout the earth that had come forth from the sons of Noah.[61] Genesis 11:1-9 (ESV) explains that after God separated the nations at the Tower of Babel, He fixed their borders according to the number of the 'sons of God'.

Because these seventy nations rejected God, He placed them under the spiritual influence of the fallen sons of God. These fallen sons are the pantheon of gods who have demonically influenced the nations over the centuries through the world religions that they empower.

Although Satan had successfully infiltrated the line of Adam, God raised Abram up in order to give the nations the opportunity to find Him through his descendants. This was realized on the day of Pentecost as 3,000 Jews from every nation responded to Peter's call.[62]

Down To Egypt:

After God called Abram he led him into the Negev to live for a season.[63] A great famine forced Abram to leave the Negev and go down to Egypt in search of food. While there, Sarai was taken into Pharaoh's household to be a part of his royal harem because Abram was too afraid to say that she was his wife.[64]

To preserve the purity of Abram's lineage and later fulfill God's word to the serpent, *"And I will put enmity between you and the woman, and between your seed and her seed; He shall bruise your head, and you shall bruise His heel;"*[65] God rescued Sarai from Pharaoh's harem by inflicting plagues upon his household. Chased from Egypt, Abram returned to Canaan a wealthy man.[66]

Giants in the Land:

Abram eventually settled in Hebron and all seemed well until a regional war broke out between two Kings.[67] What is of interest here, is that one of these kings, Chedorlaomer, attacked three giant clans:

> *"In the fourteenth year Chedorlaomer and the Kings that were with him came and attacked the Rephaim in Ashteroth Karnaim, the Zuzim in Ham, the Emim is Shaveh Kiriathaim..."*[68]

Deuteronomy 2:10-11 and 2:20-21 confirm that the fallen sons of God; who had mated with the women of the earth 20 generations back, had successfully reproduced giants throughout Canaan.[69]

> *The Emim had dwelt there in times past, a people as great and numerous and tall as the Anakim. They were also regarded as giants, like the Anakim, but the Moabites call them Emim...That was also regarded as a land of giants; gi-ants formerly dwelt there. But the Ammonites call them Zamzummim, a people as great and numerous and tall as the Anakim. But the Lord destroyed them before them, and they dispossessed them and dwelt in their place.*

CHAPTER EIGHT

Moloch and the Fallen Sons of God

Incest: The Origin of Moloch Worship:

The fallen sons of God, the pantheon of gods set over the nations, continued to pollute Canaan in advance of the Exodus and the Israelites entrance into the Promised Land. This was evident in Sodom and Gomorrah, cities that were judged by God for their extreme corruption.

> *"As I live," says the Lord God, "neither your sister Sodom nor her daughters have done as you and your daughters have done. Look, this was the iniquity of your sister Sodom: she and her daughter had pride, fullness of food, and abundance of idleness; neither did she strengthen the hand of the poor and needy. And they were haughty and committed abomination before Me; therefore*
> *I took them away as I saw fit."[70]*

Lot pitched his tent in the city of Sodom, on the Jordan plain.[71] Some time later, warned by two destroying angels, Lot gathered his family and fled Sodom because of the sinful depravity that ran rampant within its walls.[72]

Although Lot and his daughters escaped the judgment that rained down on Sodom and Gomorrah that day, they did not escape the sexual pollution that had defiled the land through the fallen sons of God.

> *Then Lot went up out of Zoar and dwelt in the mountains and his two daughters were with him; for he was afraid to dwell in Zoar. And he and his two daughters*

dwelt in a cave. Now the firstborn said to the younger, "Our father is old, and there is no man on earth to come into us as is the custom of all the earth. Come let us make our father drink wine, and we will lie with him, that we may preserve the lineage of our father." So they made their father drink wine that night. And the firstborn went in and lay with her father, and he did not know when she lay down or when she arose.[73]

The same scenario ensued the next evening as Lot's younger daughter repeated her older sister's sin.[74] Consequently, Lot's daughters bore him sons. The first was named Moab and the second Ben-Ammi. These sons of Lot became the founding fathers of the Moabite and Ammonite nations – two people groups that worshipped the fire gods, Moloch and Chemosh.[75]

Centuries later when the Israelites entered Canaan, Moloch worship or ritual child sacrifice was common practice. Children were intentionally sacrificed in the fires of Moloch in exchange for divine favor or as a misguided act of contrition.[76] Today, the terrorist group Hamas continues this despicable practice by launching missiles towards Israel from Palestinian schoolyards. Hundreds of Palestinian children have been intentionally sacrificed to influence the nations against Israel. Moloch, the fallen son of God over Israel is the ruling power behind this evil strategy.

'Moloch' means 'king' or 'ruler,' and was directly tied to the fertility god Baal.[77] On at least two occasions, the Lord spoke to Jeremiah about it:

"Because they have forsaken Me and made this an alien place, because they have burned incense in it to other gods whom neither they, their fathers, nor the kings of Judah have known, and have filled this place with the blood of the innocents (they have also built the high places of Baal, to burn their sons with fire for burnt offerings to Baal, which I did not command or speak, nor did it come into My mind)... And they built the high places of Baal which are in the Valley of the Son of Hinnom, to cause their sons and their daughters to pass through the fire to Moloch, which I did not command them, nor did it come into My mind that they should do this abomination, to cause Judah to sin."[78]

'Baal', meaning 'lord' or 'master' was the primary god of the Canaanites. Canaan as mentioned earlier was the grandson of Noah, thus making the Canaanites one of the seventy nations placed under the fallen sons of God.

When the Most High divided their inheritance to the nations, When He separated the sons of Adam, He set the boundaries of the peoples According to the number of the children of Israel.[79]

This means that Moloch and Baal were the fallen sons of God that ruled over the Canaanite people.

In addition to exchanging the lives of the next generation for plentiful crops and divine protection, the Canaanites believed that Baal could be persuaded to fertilize their land with his seed if they engaged in rampant sexual activity.[80] According to an article entitled Fertility Cults of Canaan the Canaanites practiced 'sympathetic magic,' believing they could influ-ence the gods' actions by performing the behavior they wished the gods to demonstrate. Believing that the sexual union of Baal and Asherah (the mistress of Baal) produced fertility, the Canaanites engaged in immoral sex to cause the gods to join together, thus ensuring good harvests.[81]

Not surprisingly, the capitol of Israel, Tel Aviv, is considered to be the Gay Capitol of the Middle East by the worldwide Gay Community.[82] No other Middle Eastern country is as tolerant as Israel when it comes to Gay rights. Just as Moloch spiritually empowers child sacrifice in Gaza, Baal fuels homosexual activity throughout Israel.

Possessing the Gates:[83]

When the daughters of Lot lay with their father they opened a gate, door or entry point for the fallen sons of God, Moloch and Chemosh, to legally, spiritually, and culturally shape the Moabite and Ammonite peoples.

'Doors' and 'gates' are mentioned throughout Scripture.[84] A gate is an opening into a larger space while a door is a smaller opening within the larger space. In the spiritual realm gates are large openings into the heavenly places while doors are smaller openings within the heavenly places. Abraham, Isaac and Jacob were keenly aware of the reality and importance of possessing spiritual gates and doors.[85]

Nearly two millennia after Jacob's death, Jesus stood in Caesarea Philippi and made a declaration about the gates of Hades.

> *And I also say to you that you are Peter, and on this rock I will build My church,*
> *and the gates of Hades shall not prevail against it.[86]*

What did the Patriarchs and the Lord Jesus understand about gates and doors that we can glean from today? And, is there any connection between spiritual gates and doors and the fallen sons of God?

When Jesus entered Caesarea Philippi He entered a region that is referred to today as the Golan Heights. The Golan is a fertile region sandwiched between Mount Hermon in northern Israel, with Syria to the east and the Sea of Galilee in the south.

In the days of Jesus the Golan was called Bashan[87] and was the region where the Rephaim, or giants, lived.[88] Bashan was central headquarters for these half-human, half-fallen sons of God. When Jesus declared that the gates of Ha-des would not prevail against His people he was emphatically stating that the Rephaim or their departed spirits would not be able to overcome His people.

Before screaming, "blashphemy!" read Psalm 22:12-18, which provides a prophetic snapshot of the crucifixion of Jesus and the fulfillment of the Lord's word in Genesis 3:15:

> *Many bulls (the departed spirits of the Rephaim), have surrounded Me; strong bulls of Bashan have encircled Me. They gape at Me with their mouths, like a raging and roaring lion. I am poured out like water, and all My bones are out of joint; My heart is like wax; it has melted within Me. My strength is dried up like a potsherd, and My tongue clings to My jaws; you have brought Me to the dust of death. For dogs have surrounded Me; the congregation (the Rephaim) of the wicked has enclosed Me. They pierced My hands and My feet; I can count all My bones. They look and stare at Me. They divide My garments among them, for My clothing they cast lots.*

The word 'Rephaim' means 'giants' but is also translated 'departed spirits'. When the Philistines heard that David had become King of Israel they mobilized their forces and camped outside of Jerusalem in the Valley of Rephaim.[89] This valley was also known as 'the valley of giants' or 'the valley of departed spirits'.[90]

CHAPTER NINE

Israel and the Fallen Sons of God

The Gods of Egypt:

When the Israelites entered the land of Canaan, God warned them not to allow their children to pass through the fires of Moloch.[91] Moloch was undoubtedly the chief deity, or fallen son of God, that ruled over the Canaanite people and sought to seduce the people of Israel to do the same. The Israelites were eventually swayed by the cult of Moloch and began to sacrifice their children in exchange for divine favor.[92]

It is likely that Israel fell prey to the influence of Moloch because of their prior exposure to the idols of Egypt. The Egyptians, like the Canaanites, were the direct descendants of Noah's son Ham and, more specifically, the descendants of Noah's grandson Mizram.[93] Modern Egyptians refer to themselves today as Misr, which is a derivative of Mizraim.[94]

Like the Canaanites, the Egyptians were among the seventy nations God placed under 'the fallen sons of God'.[95] Israel's familiarity and comfort with Egypt's gods influenced their decision to fashion the gold calf at Mount Sinai.

Out of Egypt:

When God delivered the Israelites from Egyptian bondage He directed Moses to pronounce ten plagues upon the ten primary gods of Egypt. These gods were both male and female:

1. Hapi, the god of the Nile River (water).
2. Heqt, the goddess of birth (frogs).
3. Geb, the god of earth (gnats).
4. Kheper, the god of beetles (flies).
5. Apis or Hathor, the sacred bull or cow god (cattle).
6. Isis, the goddess of healing (boils).
7. Nut, the goddess of the sky (hail).
8. Seth, the god of crops (locusts).
9. Ra, the sun god (darkness).
10. Pharoah, the chief god of Egypt (firstborn).[96]

The Sin at Sinai:

Exodus 32:1-4 describes how the Israelites sinned at Mount Sinai:

> Now when the people saw that Moses delayed coming down from the mountain, the people gathered together to Aaron, and said to him, "Come, make us gods that shall go before us, for as for this Moses, the man who brought us up out of the land of Egypt, we do not know what has become of him."
>
> And Aaron said to them, "Break off the golden earrings which are in the ears of your wives, your sons and your daughters, and bring them to Me." So all the people broke off the golden earrings, which were in their ears and brought them to Aaron. And he received the gold from their hand, and he fashioned it with an engraving tool, and made a molded calf.
>
> Then they said, "This is your god, O Israel, that brought you out of the land of Egypt!"

God had delivered Israel from Egyptian bondage and strategically positioned them at the foot of Mount Sinai. His heart was to gather His people, reveal Himself as their Father, and establish a covenant relationship with them that would endure through time. The Israelites, however, did not accept God's invitation to draw near because they had the spirit of slavery.

For 430 years the children of Israel had been told what to do, and when to do it! Their basic needs, including housing, food and clothing were provided; but they had no paradigm for what it meant to be fathered, let alone trust a divine being they could not see. Conditioned by the idolatrous culture that enveloped them in Egypt and the fear of being punished by their taskmasters, their ability to trust God was weak at best. Little did they understand the short and long term consequences of forsaking God for the calf idol of Egypt.[97]

Star Wars:

Stephen, a man full of God's grace and power,[98] stood before the high council of Jerusalem (the Sanhedrin) to present, in great detail, a series of biblical and historical proofs that traced Israel's early history from Abraham to Jesus as Messiah.[99]

During this powerful presentation of the facts, Stephen mentioned the golden calf and its relationship to star worship. Let's pick up the story in Acts 7:38-43:

> *This is he (Moses) who was in the congregation in the wilderness with the Angel who spoke to him on Mount Sinai, and with our fathers, the one who received the living oracles to give to us, whom our fathers would not obey, but rejected. And in their hearts they turned back to Egypt, saying to Aaron, "Make us gods to go before us; as for this Moses who brought us out of the land of Egypt, we do not know what has become of him. And they made a calf in those days, offered sac-rifices to the idol, and rejoiced in the work of their own hands. Then God turned and gave them up to worship the host of heaven, as it is written in the book of the*
> *Prophets: 'Did you offer Me slaughtered animals and sacrifices during forty years in the wilderness, O house of Israel? You also took up the tabernacle of Moloch, and the star of your Remphan (Saturn), images which you made to worship; and*
> *I will carry you away before Babylon.'"*

According to Stephen's defense, Israel continued to worship the golden calf (Moloch) in the wilderness years as well as dabbling in star worship. Knowing that the nations that lived in Canaan were star worshippers God warned Israel, through Moses, not to be seduced as they were at Mount Sinai.

> *And take heed, lest you lift your eyes to heaven, when you see the sun, the moon, and the stars, all the host of heaven, you feel driven to worship them and serve them, which the Lord your God has given to all the peoples under the whole heaven as a heritage.[100]*

In other words, God placed all the people—the nations—under the spiritual influence of the moon, stars and host of heaven as a heritage. Note the similarity with Deuteronomy 32:8, which tells us that God placed the seventy nations scattered at the Tower of Babel under the spiritual influence of the fallen sons of God as their inheritance.

Stars are mentioned throughout Scripture. Not just as celestial entities in the heavens, but as high-level spiritual beings. In Isaiah 14:12-14, Lucifer attempted to exalt his throne above the stars of God.

36

How you are fallen from heaven, O Lucifer, son of the morning! How you are cut down to the ground, You who weakened the nations! For you have said in your heart: "I will ascend into heaven, I will exalt my throne above the stars of God; I will also sit on the mount of the congregation On the farthest sides of the north; I will ascend above the heights of the clouds, I will be like the Most High."

And, looking to Judges 5:20, we see that the stars fought against the Canaanite King Sisera:

They fought from the heavens; The stars from their courses fought against Sisera.

Next we find in Revelation 9:1-2 that authority is entrusted to a star to open the bottomless pit:

Then the fifth angel sounded: And I saw a star fallen from heaven to the earth. To him was given the key to the bottomless pit. And he opened the bottomless pit, and smoke arose out of the pit like the smoke of a great furnace. So the sun and the air were darkened because of the smoke of the pit.

Given all of this we must ask, "Are the stars a type of fallen sons of God? And, if not, what is their relationship to Moloch? Scripture indicates that there is a definite connection between Moloch and star worship. Zephaniah 1:4-6 provides insight:

I will stretch out My hand against Judah, and against all the inhabitants of Jerusalem. I will cut off every trace of Baal from this place, the names of the idolatrous priests with the pagan priests – those who worship the host of heaven (stars) on the housetops, those who worship and swear by Milcom (Moloch); those who have turned back from following the Lord, and have not sought nor inquired of Him.

If Moloch is a fallen son of God, as we proposed earlier, then the unrighteous stars are high-level spiritual beings that work in tandem with Moloch to defile the lands in which the nations reside.[101]

Bad Report:

Israel wandered for forty years in the wilderness worshipping Moloch and the star god, Saturn, because they did not have the capacity to possess what God wanted to entrust to them. Enslaved for 430 years, they functioned according to the spirit of slavery instead of the spirit of sonship. Brainwashed by the Egyptians, they had learned to survive day to day and had no understanding of

37

inheritance or how to rule and reign.

Numbers 13:1-3 gives the account of how God sent twelve men, one leader from each of the twelve tribes of Israel, into the land of Canaan to explore for future conquest. Forty days later the twelve returned and reported their perceptions. Two of the twelve Joshua and Caleb, spoke as sons but the other ten spoke as if they were slaves.

> *We went to the land where you (Moses) sent us. It truly flows with milk and honey, and this is its fruit. Nevertheless the people who dwell in the land are strong; the cities are fortified and very large; moreover we saw the descendants of Anak (Giants) there. The Amalekites dwell in the land of the South; the Hit-tites, the Jebusites, and the Amorites dwell in the mountains; and the Canaanites dwell by the sea and along the banks of the Jordan.*
>
> *Then Caleb quieted the people before Moses, and said, "Let us go up at once and take possession, for we are well able to overcome it." But the men who had gone up with him said, "We are not able to go up against the people for they are stronger than we," And they gave the children of Israel a bad report of the land which they had spied out saying, "The land through which we have gone as spies is a land that devours its inhabitants, and all the people whom we saw in it are men of great stature. There we saw the giants (the descendants of Anak came from the giants); and we are grasshoppers in our own sight, and so we were in their sight."[102]*

The descendants of the fallen sons of God and the women of the earth had infiltrated the land of Canaan according to plan, and were so enormous that their size struck fear deep into the hearts of Israel. Blinded, the Israelites declared that what God had promised them could not be achieved. Just as they had shrunk back at Mount Sinai, they again refused to draw near to the Lord. Their lack of vision and trust would cost them forty years in the wilderness.

Divine Orders: *Seek and Destroy*

Orphans, those who function according to the spirit of slavery, do not believe that God loves them or that He desires to give them an inheritance (something tangible they have not earned). Moses' generation did not trust God, even though He had performed great miracles in Egypt on their behalf and parted the Red Sea during the Exodus.

After forty years of purging the Israelites of their slave mindsets, God gave them the toughest marching orders imaginable. Before you enter the promise land, seek out the giants of the surrounding nations and destroy them completely!

> *Hear, O Israel: You are to cross over the Jordan today, and go in to dispossess nations greater and mightier than yourself, cities great and fortified up to heaven, a people great and tall, the descendants of the Anakim, whom you know, and of whom you heard it said, "Who can stand before the descendants of Anak?" Therefore understand today that the Lord your God is He who goes over before you as a consuming fire. He will destroy them and bring them down before you; so you shall drive them out and destroy them quickly, as the Lord has said to you.[103]*

Joshua and a new generation of Israelites who had been set free from the spirit of slavery prepared themselves to enter the land of Canaan.

A Modern-day Correlation:

On May 2, 2011 Osama bin-Laden the founder and head of the militant group al-Qaeda was killed in Pakistan by special U.S. forces.[104] Before the announcement of bin-Laden's death was made official, rumors spread quickly through the media prompting large crowds to gather outside the White House, Ground Zero, the Pentagon and Times Square to celebrate.

Like Osama bin-Laden, the descendants of the fallen sons of God and the women of the earth (known as the Nephilim, Anakim and Rephaim) were agents of great evil[105] who perpetuated terrible acts of violence against the nation of Israel as well as any who supported them. God's orders to kill and destroy these giant enclaves were not the orders of a cruel God who wanted to murder innocent people; but the orders of a just, righteous and benevolent God who was intent on protecting His people and bringing forth the Second Adam to bruise the serpent's head.

Jericho: *City of the Moon*

As a boy I loved a television show that featured an expert billiards player named 'Minnesota Fats.' What I enjoyed most about Rudolph Wanderone,[106] Fats' actual name, was that he had perfected the ability to strategically position the cue ball after making a great shot so he could make another great shot. Like Fats, God 'strategically' positioned His people on the plains of Jericho for His next move.

When we understand that Jericho was the seat of moon worship in Canaan, it is easy to see why God wanted it destroyed. God's plan was strategic: remove

39

the chief center of demonic power in the land, and all the other cities in Canaan would fall like dominoes. Jericho's destruction was so vital for the future conquest of Canaan that God dispatched the Commander of the host, the army of the Lord to help Israel take the city.

> *And it came to pass, when Joshua was by Jericho, that he lifted his eyes and looked, and behold, a Man stood opposite him with His sword drawn in His hand. And Joshua went to Him and said to Him, "Are You for us or for our adversaries?"*
>
> *So He said, "No, but as Commander of the army of the Lord I have now come."*
>
> *And Joshua fell on his face to the earth and worshiped, and said to Him, "What does my Lord say to His servant?"*
>
> *Then the Commander of the Lord's army said to Joshua, "Take your sandal off your foot, for the place where you stand is holy." And Joshua did so.[107]*

Jericho was the first city that the Israelites conquered. Why? There were two reasons: First, Jericho was the eastern gateway into Israel, and according to Ezekiel 43:1-4, the Glory of God rises first in the East. Secondly, 'Jericho' or 'The City of the Moon'[108] meant that Jericho was the spiritual center for star worship in the land of Canaan. The male moon god, Yerah, was the chief god of the Canaanite pantheon and the female sun-god, Shamash, was his consort. Later, the names of these moon gods would be changed to Baal and Asteroth.[109]

The Babylonian Garment:

After the walls of Jericho fell[110] the Israelites destroyed all that was in the city, including all the men, women and children, except Rahab and her family.[111] As directed by God, they burned Jericho to the ground. Phase One of the con-quest of Canaan was complete.

Riding high after their victory at Jericho, Joshua sent 3,000 men to attack the city of Ai.[112] But, to their great surprise, instead of taking the city they were badly defeated. Joshua 7:10-12 explains why:

> *So the Lord said to Joshua: "Get up! Why do you lie thus on your face? Israel has sinned, and they have also transgressed my covenant, which I commanded them. For they have even taken some of the accursed things, and have both stolen and deceived; and they have put it among their own stuff. Therefore the children of Israel could not stand before their enemies, but turned their backs before their*

40

enemies, because they have become doomed to destruction. Neither will I be with you anymore, unless you destroy the accursed from among you."

What were the accursed things? Joshua 7:21 mentions three items that Achan had coveted for himself; a Babylonian garment, two hundred shekels of silver, and a wedge of gold weighing fifty shekels. It is hard to imagine why the Lord viewed a simple garment and some precious metals as accursed, but further study reveals that it wasn't the precious metals that upset the Lord, but the Babylonian garment.

When Moses, along with the elders of Israel, delivered God's commands to the people, he clearly outlined the curses that would come upon them if they chose not to walk in His ways.[113] Scripture is clear that God does not ignore such sinful behavior:

> *Do not be deceived, God is not mocked; for whatever a man sows, that he will also reap.*[114]

Why would a seemingly harmless garment from Babylon be so offensive to God that He would remove His protection from His people and allow them to be defeated? The answer can be traced to the nation of Babylon.

Babylon was founded by Nimrod, the great-grandson of Noah,[115] and the name, 'Babylon,' means 'gateway of the god.'[116] Centuries later Terah, the father of Abraham, moved his family to a city called Ur, also known as 'the city of the moon.'[117] Later, Terah uprooted his family from Ur and settled in Haran, the site of the temple of the moon-god Sin.[118]

Like the calf idol at Mount Sinai, the primary symbol of the moon god Sin was a bull with a horizontal crescent of the waking moon placed between its horns.[119] Abram, who would later be named Abraham, had been a long-time resident of Babylon, meaning that he himself had been a moon worshipper.[120]

Israel's generational line was rooted in moon worship. Throughout their history, God's people were drawn by the alluring influence of celestial worship. This is why Moses warned the Israelites not to worship the sun, moon or stars[121] and why the Lord designated Jericho and all of its accursed things for destruction.

Achan did not heed God's command to keep away from the accursed items of Jericho.[122] As a consequence, the Israelites were routed at Ai.

CHAPTER TEN

Generational Relevance of the Fallen Sons of God in Israel

David and Goliath:

The account of David and Goliath is widely known and accepted as one of the great stories of all time. Goliath, as most know, was a Philistine warrior of enormous size and strength.[123] But what many do not know is that Goliath was an Anakim – a hybrid mixture of man and an elohim or 'fallen son' of God.[124]

The name 'Goliath' has two possible meanings: First, it may mean to uncover, remove or go into exile. It can also be rendered as the revealing of someone, a secret or message.[125] Based on the second definition, is it possible that we have viewed Goliath only as the Philistine giant slain by David and missed a greater revelation?

1 Samuel 17:54 informs us that after David killed Goliath he took his head and brought it to Jerusalem. 'Yara', from which the first half of the word 'Jerusalem' is derived, means to cast, direct or instruct as in 'the way to go through.' And, 'Shalem', the second half of the word 'Jerusalem', means to be made complete; to make amends; restitution or restore.[126] When 'Yara' and 'Shalem' are joined they comprise the word 'Y'rn-sha-lah-yim,' meaning the place where God informs mankind that He has made a way for them to be restored to Him

through the Second Adam – Jesus Christ.[127]

Jewish tradition tells us that after David brought Goliath's head to Jerusalem he buried it at Golgatha – the 'place of the skull.' Is it possible that Goliath's skull is buried at Golgatha? And what correlation, if any, does this have with Goliath being a 'fallen son of God'?

Jesus came and fulfilled what the first Adam failed to do – He defeated God's enemies at the gates of Hades.[128] Not coincidentally, David defeated the arch-enemy of Israel a thousand years earlier, recaptured the Ark of the Covenant, and buried Goliath's head at the exact site where Jesus would restore mankind to the Father.[129]

Fractal Patterns:

A fractal is defined as a '…rough or fragmented geometrical shape that can be subdivided in parts, each of which is (at least approximately) a smaller copy of the whole.'[130] The Fractal Foundation defines a fractal more simply as a "… never ending pattern."[131]

From the Babylonian city of Haran, where Abram worshipped the moon god Sin; to Mount Sinai, where the Israelites worshipped the golden calf; to the Mount of Olives in Jerusalem, where Solomon built pagan shrines for child sacrifice to Chemosh and Moloch;[132] the people of Israel broke covenant with God. The consequences of this covenant breaking fractal pattern eventually led to Israel's demise and exile to foreign nations.[133]

In an attempt to turn the tide, God raised up prophets like Jeremiah to call His people back to their first love and to warn them of the terrible consequences of violating covenant relationship with Him for other gods.[134] Sadly, this message fell on deaf ears and the fractal pattern of covenant breaking continued on from one generation to the next.

The Golden Calves:

When most people break covenant with God they are unaware of the far-reaching consequences of their actions. This was the case when David took Uriah's wife for himself in a moment of lust filled passion.[135]

Years later, David's son Solomon succumbed to the same sexual temptations but on a much greater scale![136] His decision to build altars for his wives' foreign gods opened the door for Baal worship to take deeper root in the heart of Israel.

After Solomon died, his son Rehoboam succeeded him as king.[137] His reign was short lived as God ripped away from him ten of the twelve tribes of Israel, entrusting them to a man named Jeroboam.[138] Fearing that the ten tribes he now ruled would go back to Jerusalem to worship the Lord, Jeroboam implemented an ancient solution – Baal worship (the golden calves):

> *And Jeroboam said in his heart, "Now the kingdom may return to the house of David: If these people go up to offer sacrifices in the house of the Lord at Jerusalem, then the heart of this people will turn back to their Lord, Rehoboam King of Judah, and they will kill me and go back to Rehoboam King of Judah."*
>
> *Therefore the King asked advice, made two calves of gold and said to the people, "It is too much for you to go up to Jerusalem. Here are your gods, O Israel, which brought you from the land of Egypt!"[139]*

Jeroboam's decision to station the golden calves at Dan and Bethel[140] broke covenant with God, setting the stage for the rise of Jezebel and the prophets of Baal.

Baal worship is first mentioned in the Bible in Numbers 25:1-4 when men from the camp of Israel were seduced by Moabite women into engaging in sexual activity while making sacrifices to their god – the Baal of Peor. As a consequence, the sons of Israel were joined in sprit, soul and body to the Moabite women and to the Baal of Peor himself.

This raises the question: Who was Baal?

Baal was the name of the supreme god worshipped in ancient Canaan and Phoenicia. The practice of Baal worship infiltrated Jewish religious life during the time of Judges (Judges 3:7), became widespread in Israel during the reign of Ahab (1 Kings 16:31-33) and also affected Judah (2 Chronicles 28:1-2). The word Baal means 'lord'; the plural is Baalim. In sum, Baal was a fertility god who was believed to enable the earth to produce crops and people to produce children. Baal worship was rooted in sensuality and involved ritualistic prostitution in the temples. At times, appeasing Baal required human sacrifice, usually the firstborn of the one making the sacrifice (Jeremiah 19:5).[141]

Baal was, and continues to be, the archenemy of God's people. In addition to being synonymous with Moloch,[142] Baal was also called Apollo, Jupiter, Nimrod and Saturn to name a few.[143]

Like the kings who preceded him, Ahab worshipped the golden calves erected by Jeroboam; but with one significant difference – he married Jezebel, the daughter of King Ethbaal of the Sidonians.[144] Ahab's alliance with Jezebel's father, also known as the King of Tyre,[145] provoked the Lord to such great anger that He decreed a nationwide famine upon Israel through the prophet Elijah.[146] God's judgment fell upon the land because Ahab had opened the spiritual gates of Israel to the demonic influence of Baal at a level not seen before.

The name Jezebel means, "Where is the Prince?' It was a 'ritual cry' from worship ceremonies that honored Baal, the Prince of the Underworld.[147] During her tenure as the 'First Lady' of Israel Jezebel attempted to kill the prophets of God while raising up 450 prophets of Baal and 400 prophets of Asherah.[148]

Divine Confrontation:

In 2008 my oldest son, Jordan, and I visited Israel. One of the highlights of our trip was visiting Mount Carmel, the site where the prophet Elijah defeated the prophets of Baal and Asherah.[149] Baal, the supreme deity of the Canaanite people, was worshipped for one primary purpose – rainfall. Because Israel was, and still is today, an arid land, rain was crucial for a successful harvest. In 1 Kings 17:1 we see that Elijah decreed there would be no rainfall and the rain stopped, setting the stage for a confrontation between the followers of Jezebel and Elijah. In an amazing display of divine power, the fire of God fell upon the altar that Elijah had built establishing the supremacy of the Lord over Baal.[150]

Soon after, God released the heavens and the 3½-year drought ended.[151] Baal worship was fueled by rampant sexual immorality and child sacrifice. When these two elements of covenant breaking were removed from God's people, His blessing was restored.

Healing The Land:

From the start, we have attempted to establish biblical and historical evidence that supports the theory that the fallen sons of God infiltrated the land of Canaan both physically and spiritually to pollute the gene pool of Israel, war with her people, and block the coming Messiah. We have also maintained that Satan was, and is, a fallen son of God who convinced other sons of God to mate with the women of the earth.

45

Michael Heiser, a consultant for Logos Bible Software, says that the Hebrew word for earth 'eres' is also rendered in certain contexts of the Bible as 'Sheol' or 'the Underworld'.[152] Isaiah 14:12-15 adds that the star of the morning, identified as Lucifer in the KJV, once attempted to exalt his throne above the stars of God, but God threw him down to earth (the Underworld).

If Satan is a fallen son of God and was thrown to earth to rule the Underworld, then it is clear that his strategy was to fight Israel on the ground through the gods of the surrounding nations.[153]

Prior to entering the Promised land Moses made it explicitly clear that if the Israelites succumbed to the sexual practices of the Canaanite people and sacrificed their children in the fires of Moloch, God would spit them out!

> *Do not defile yourselves with any of these things; for by all these the nations are defiled, which I am casting out before you. For the land is defiled; therefore I visit the punishment of its iniquity upon it, and the land vomits out its inhabit-ants. You shall therefore keep My statutes and My judgments, and shall not commit any of these abominations, either any of your own nation or any stranger who dwells among you (for all these abominations the men of the land have done, who were before you, and thus the land is defiled), lest the land vomit you out also when you defile it, as it vomited out the nations that were before you. For whoever commits any of these abominations, the persons who commit them shall be cut off from among their people.[154]*

When a generation sacrifices its children in exchange for protection, prosperity or convenience, it opens the door for the spirit of death to destroy future generations. Likewise, when a generation condones and practices aberrant forms of sexuality outside the covenant of marriage, it defiles future generations and opens the door for the spirit of rebellion.

CHAPTER ELEVEN

Generational Relevance of the Sons of God Today

I received an email in early 2013 from Paul Cox that offered profound insight regarding Malachi 4:5-6, which states:

> *Behold, I will send you Elijah the prophet Before the coming of the great and dreadful day of the L*ord. *And he will turn the hearts of the fathers to the children, and the hearts of the children to their fathers, lest I come and strike the earth with a curse.*

Paul wrote:

> *"It was the intent of the Lord that sexual intercourse between two people would be within the covenant and safety of marriage. At that time a person would no longer be under the authority of their father and mother and would be joined to their spouse. This is a spiritual principle that affects a person's spirit, soul and body. By contrast, if sexual intercourse between two individuals occurred while still under their parents' roof, the person would likewise no longer be under their parents' authority and would be joined to their partner. As a result, the individual would have cause to rebel against their parents' authority, as their spirit would recognize that they were joined to someone else. Does Elijah come to turn the hearts of the children back to their fathers and vice versa to deal with this issue?"*

When the spirit of Elijah supernaturally turns the hearts of fathers back to the children and vice versa it is much more than an act of reconciliation. When the Malachi 4:5-6 prophecy goes into effect, a spiritual breakthrough occurs that removes from a person's generational line both the toxic slime of Moloch and Baal and the spirit of witchcraft that resulted from rebelling against their parents' authority. Luke 1:15-17 confirms this:

> For he (John the Baptist) will be great in the sight of the Lord, and shall drink neither wine nor strong drink. He will also be filled with the Holy Spirit, even from his mother's womb. And he will turn many of the children of Israel to the Lord their God. He will also go before Him in the spirit and power of Elijah to turn the hearts of the fathers to the children, and the disobedient (those who are rebellious) to the wisdom of the just, to make ready a people prepared for the Lord.

Is it possible that when parents repent to their children for their own sexual sins that revival will follow? If so, this means that parents will need to dialogue openly and honestly about their sexual past. When the spirit of Elijah moves, God will begin to heal the land.

The Bulls of Bashan:

In the section entitled 'Possessing the Gates', I briefly alluded to Jesus' declaration at Caesarea Philippi that the gates of Hades would not prevail against the church, and that the bulls to which the Psalmist referred in Psalm 22:12-13 were the Rephaim or departed spirits of the chief leaders of the earth.[155]

The Hebrew word 'repai'm' is translated as ghosts of the dead; shades; the sunken ones or those who dwell in the netherworld:[156, 157]

> Hell (Sheol) is excited about you, to meet you at your coming; it stirs up the dead (Rephaim) for you, all the chief ones of the earth; it has raised up from their thrones all the kings of the nations. They all speak and say to you: "Have you also become as weak as we? Have you become like us? Your pomp is brought down to Sheol, and the sound of your stringed instruments; the maggot is spread under you, and worms cover you."[158]

When the Hebrew Bible was translated into Greek in ancient Alexandria around 200 BC, the word 'Hades' (the Greek Underworld) was substituted for Sheol.[159] When Jesus arrived in Caesarea Philippi, which was located in the region of Bashan, and declared that the gates of Hades would not prevail against the church, He was saying that the Rephaim who lived in the Nether-world (Hades or Sheol) would not be able to stop His church from advancing.

In his article, "The Nachash and His Seed," Michael Heiser unlocks the meaning of the word Bashan:

> The place name 'Bashan' is spelled 'Batham' meaning 'serpent' – Bashan was the 'place of the serpent.'[160]

This brings us full circle to Genesis 3:14-15 where we learned that the serpent, or 'nachash' (the Hebrew adjective for 'shining one') was told that Eve's Seed would bruise his head.[161]

If Bashan is translated 'serpent' then who are the 'cows' of Bashan that are referred to in Amos 4:1? Amos 3:14 provides the first clue:

> *That in the day I punish Israel for their transgressions, I will also visit destruc-tion on the altars of Bethel, and the horns of the altar shall be cut off and fall to the ground.*

Amos 8:6 offers a second clue:

> *Those who swear by the sin of Samaria, who say, "As your god lives, O Dan!"*

1 Kings 12:28-31 tells us that Jeroboam set up two golden calves, one in Bethel and one in Dan:

> *Then King Rehoboam sent Adoram, who was in charge of the revenue; but all Israel stoned him with stones, and he died. Therefore King Rehoboam mounted his chariot in haste to flee to Jerusalem. So Israel has been in rebellion against the house of David to this day.*

> *Now it came to pass when all Israel heard that Jeroboam had come back, they sent for him and called him to the congregation, and made him king over all Israel. There was none who followed the house of David, but the tribe of Judah only.*

> *And when Rehoboam came to Jerusalem, he assembled all the house of Judah with the tribe of Benjamin, one hundred and eighty thousand chosen men who were warriors, to fight against the house of Israel, that he might restore the king-dom to Rehoboam the son of Solomon.*

Next, Judges 18:30-31 reveals that the tribe of Dan set up a carved image when they entered the Promise Land:

> *Then the children of Dan set up for themselves the carved image; and Jonathan the son of Gershom, the son of Manasseh, and his sons were priests to the tribe of Dan until the day of the captivity of the land. So they set up for themselves Micah's carved image which he made, all the time that the house of God was in Shiloh.*

49

Deuteronomy 33:22 provides a final clue:

Dan is a lion's whelp (cub); he shall leap from Bashan.

So what can we conclude about the cows of Bashan? They were the fallen sons of god that demonically undergirded Baal worship in Israel, and were the spiritual powers that encircled Jesus while He hung on the cross, as prophesied in Psalm 22:12-13:

Many bulls have surrounded Me; Strong bulls of Bashan have encircled Me. They gape at Me with their mouths, Like a raging and roaring lion.

CHAPTER TWELVE

The Revealed sons of God

All of Creation Waits:

> *For the earnest expectation of the creation eagerly awaits for the revealing of the sons of God.*[162]

In the fall of October 2001, I hopped on a plane and headed to Buenos Aires with a contingent of people from Hawaii to attend Harvest Evangelism's annual City Reaching Conference. During a conference break I ventured out into the heart of the Buenos Aires shopping district with two friends in search of a prized Argentine leather jacket. As my friends and I walked from shop to shop, we met a prophetically gifted woman from a local evangelist's ministry.

After sharing a word of encouragement with one of my friends she turned to me, while rocking her arms back and forth as if she was cradling a baby and said, "You, you! You're God's bambino (baby)! God loves you!" Immediately, the presence of God covered me like a warm blanket and tears ran down my cheek.

Prior to this encounter with God I did not have the revelation that I was God's bambino. My walk with God had been filled with striving and was performance based, which led only to burn out and fatigue. In the midst of my downward spiral, my Heavenly Father graciously revealed that I was His beloved child!

Before the Fall, Adam and Eve experienced what it meant to be God's son and daughter as they basked in the glow of their Father's ever-present affection. By design, Satan drew Adam and Eve away from the security of their Father's loving arms and convinced them to eat from the tree of knowledge of good and evil. Immediately, three changes occurred: first, they became estranged from the Father as their gaze shifted from Him onto themselves. Second, they lost the experiential knowledge of God's embrace – that they were His precious son and daughter.[163] And third, they became estranged from the heavenly realms and lost sight of their supernatural position that God originally gave to them as the sons of God.

Ephesians 1:3-6 explains that although sin altered the First Couple's relationship with God their standing, or position, with Him did not change:

> *Blessed be the God and Father of our Lord Jesus Christ, who has blessed us with every spiritual blessing in the heavenly places in Christ, just as he chose us in Him before the foundation of the world, that we should be holy and without blame before Him in love, having predestined us to 'adoption as sons' by Jesus Christ to Himself, according to the good pleasure of His will, to the praise of the glory of His grace, by which He made us accepted in the Beloved.*

The NIV renders Ephesians 1:5 as adoption to sonship through Jesus Christ. The Greek word for adoption is 'Huiothesia',[164] and is best translated as 'son-ship', referring to the standing or position of a son who has the rights and privileges of inheritance.[165] However, Huiothesia is rendered by the majority of Bible translators as adoption as sons conveying the idea that we become sons once we have received Jesus into our hearts (versus always having been sons).

We have always been and will always be God's sons and daughters. This has been our position, or standing, as predetermined by the Father before the foundation of the world. We are sons, but we still need to become God's children by receiving Jesus into our hearts.

> *But as many as received Him, to them He gave the right to become children of God, to those who believe in His name.*[166]

Sonship is a state of position not salvation.[167] We are reconciled to the Father when we receive the Son. Sonship grants us the authority to release the Kingdom of God on earth.[168]

Romans 8:19 tells us that all of creation, the earth, is waiting expectantly for the revealing of the sons of God. The Greek word for 'expectantly' is 'apokaradokia', meaning 'to wait with the head raised and the eye fixed on that point of the horizon from which the expected object is to come'. This definition depicts the creation as if standing on tiptoe as it eagerly waits for the people of God to embrace their standing, authority and privileges as the pre-determined sons and daughters of God.[169]

When we receive the Son of God into our hearts we not only become God's children, but we also re-activate our kingdom rights and privileges as the sons of God that were bestowed on us before the foundation of the world. Many of us know that we are God's children but few of us know that we are sons and daughters.

Let's revisit Romans 8:14-17, 19:

For those who are led by the Spirit of God, are the children of God. The Spirit you received does not make you slaves, so that you live in fear again; rather, the Spirit you received brought about your adoption to sonship. And by him we cry,
"Abba, Father." The Spirit himself testifies with our spirit that we are God's children. Now if we are children, then we are heirs — heirs of God and co-heirs with Christ...For the creation waits in eager expectation (leans forward) for the children (sons and daughters) of God to be revealed.

We Are About To Be Revealed:

The Greek word for 'revealing', 'apokalupsis', simply means disclosure. It can also be translated as appearing, coming, enlighten, make naked or uncover.[170] Apokalupsis has to do with the exposing of something that has been hidden from view, or bringing into the light that which has been kept in obscurity. In this passage it is clear that what has been hidden and held in obscurity are the sons of God! The revelation of sonship has been hidden from the church but this is about to change.[171]

The Sons of God:

What does the title 'the sons of God' mean? For the word 'sons' Paul chose the Greek word 'huios' rather than the word 'brephos' (which means infant) or 'teknon' (which describes an adolescent). The huios are mature, fully developed sons who have come of age into full maturity. The revealing of the sons of God will not be the uncovering of God's sons as infants (brephos), or as adolescents (teknon), but as those who have come to the full stature of Christ.[172]

It should also be noted that 'sons of God' is not a gender-specific term, and women are also 'sons' and enjoy 'sonship'. It is only for clarity in the politically-correct climate of our culture, that we often say, "sons and daughters".

Sonship:

As previously noted, the Greek word for sonship, 'Huiothesia', means 'Son Placement', indicating the time when a male child reached what was considered the age of maturity (somewhere around 30). At this time, the father of the young man would place his hand on the head of his son and openly proclaim, "This is my beloved son in whom I am well pleased! I bestow upon him now all of my riches and power and authority so that he might act on my behalf in all of my affairs."[173] Isn't it interesting that these are the very words spoken to Jesus by the Father after His baptism?[174]

The Five Fold:

Ephesians 4:11-13 tells us how the Lord plans to bring the sons of God (that's us) to maturity:

> *And He gave the apostles, the prophets, the evangelists, the shepherds and teachers, to equip the saints for the work of ministry, for building up the body of Christ, until we all attain to the unity of the faith and of the knowledge of the Son of God, to mature manhood, to the measure of the stature of the fullness of Christ...*

The fivefold officers of the church (Apostles, Prophets, Evangelists, Pastors, Teachers) have been given to the family of God to build up the church until:

1. We are unified
2. We understand how to function as sons like the Son of Man
3. We are mature

More than ever before we have been coming together in unity to pray for our cities, states and nations as the Lord has been supernaturally unifying us. Second, God has been transforming the body of Christ from an orphanage into a family of sons and daughters. This has been the most challenging phase of God's master plan to mature us because we have had to overcome the pains and hurts of our childhood and persevere through our trials and challenges.

Maturity:

It is God's desire to reveal us as His mature sons and daughters. This raises two important questions; what is maturity, and how will we know when we have become mature?

In John 5:19 Jesus said,

"Very truly I tell you, the Son can do nothing by himself; he can do only what he sees his Father doing, because whatever the Father does the Son also does."

I shared earlier that sonship, or Huiothesia, means son placement, indicating the time when a Roman father bestowed upon his son all of his riches, power and authority so that he might act on his behalf regarding all of his affairs. When Jesus ministered to the Jewish people He did so as a Son carrying out His Father's business. In John 4:34 Jesus said,

"My food is to do the will of Him who sent me and to accomplish His work."

The telltale sign that a believer is spiritually mature is that he (or she) desires, more than anything, to do his (or her) Heavenly Father's will.

This raises another question: How do we know what the Father is doing so we are able to carry out His will? The answer can be found in Hebrews 5:14:

But solid food is for the mature, who because of practice have their senses trained to discern good and evil.

Solid food, doing the will of God, is for the mature because they know how to discern what the Father is doing and join Him.

Exciting Times Lie Ahead!

The Father is transitioning us out of adolescence into maturity by releasing the gift of discernment in significantly greater measure so we can know what He is doing and do the greater works that Jesus spoke of in John 14:12,

"Most assuredly, I say to you, he who believes in Me, the works that I do he will do also; and greater works than these he will do, because I go to My Father."

As the adolescent season we are presently going through draws to a close, let us determine in our hearts to move on from the hurts of our childhood (anger, rejection, shame, etc.) so that the Father can bestow upon us the multiplied blessings of sonship (authority, power, heavenly resources) that He predestined us for before the foundation of the world, and fulfill the Great Com-mission!

Blessed be the God and Father of our Lord Jesus Christ, who has blessed us

with every spiritual blessing in the heavenly places in Christ, just as He chose us in Him before the foundation of the world, that we should be holy and without blame before Him in love, having predestined us to adoption as sons by Jesus Christ to Himself, according to the good pleasure of His will, to the praise of the glory of His grace, by which He made us accepted in the Beloved.[175]

CHAPTER THIRTEEN

The Foundational Gate

Two Hurricanes:

Hurricane Iselle was the strongest tropical cyclone to make landfall on the Big Island of Hawaii in recorded history. The eleventh named storm of the annual hurricane season in 2014, Iselle developed from an area of disturbed weather southwest of Mexico on July 31, and continued strengthening progressed for several days up until August 4, when Iselle reached peak intensity with maximum sustained winds of 140 mph, making it a Category 4 hurricane. As Iselle approached the Hawaiian Islands, it encountered hostile environmental conditions causing the storm to quickly weaken before making landfall on the Big Island on August 7 as a tropical storm of moderate intensity.[176]

Of special interest about this storm was both its name and the time it arrived. 'Iselle' has two possible meanings: The first definition is of Hebrew origin and means 'devoted to God'.[177] The other definition is of Turkish origin, meaning 'moonlight', 'moonbeam' or 'moon like'.[178]

As noted in an earlier chapter, Jericho, the city of the moon, was the center of moon worship in Canaan when the Israelites entered the Promise land. With that in mind, the time of Iselle's arrival was intriguing as it came more than a month before a major youth conference in Honolulu that was to address the issue of sexual purity. So what's the point? It is that Iselle was a clear sign of God's intent to deal with Moloch (symbolized by the moon) and Baal (the fallen son of God behind sexual impurity).

A second storm, Julio, followed closely behind Iselle; threatening Hawaii for the first time with the threat of back-to-back hurricanes. The name 'Julio' is of Spanish origin and means 'downy-bearded, soft haired, implying youthful', and is generally used as a boy's name.[179]

Could it be that two hurricanes, one symbolizing the moon and the other sym-bolizing the youth, were sent by God to foretell what was coming? Wonder-ing, I contacted several individuals that I knew who had a proven track record of hearing God's voice, and asked them to seek the Lord regarding the two hurricanes headed toward Hawaii.

In response to my query, a prophetic intercessor named Persis Tiner forward-ed a prophetic poem to Paul Cox, who then passed it on to me. As I read the poem, I said to myself, "You can't make this up!"

> *Hurricanes, hurricanes The winds are blowing Repent; repent*
> *For the time is here For cleansing and life*
> *No more filth of adulterous life*
> *My call is for purity A cleansing must come*
> *Do it before calamity comes.*

Persis then added, "I can't put my finger on a specific name for the repentance, but it may have to do with the concept of family life. Maybe Rob would have a better idea, and, of course, I could be off."

The Family Gate:

In recent years there has been a lot of discussion about marketplace gates (i.e. government gate, media gate, religion gate, education gate; youth gate, business gate, etc.) and the Seven Mountains.[180] This revelation has birthed ministries locally, nationally, and across the globe as the Body of Christ has increasingly realized that ministry is not confined within the four walls of the church.

Obviously, there is one gate that is foundational to all of the other gates—the family gate. Instability in our homes during our childhood leads to instability in our lives later in life, often limiting our ability to achieve our God-given potential and function as God's sons and daughters. Malachi 4:5-6 explains that the spirit of Elijah comes to deal with this foundational issue.

> *Behold, I will send you Elijah the prophet before the coming of the great and dreadful day of the Lord. And he will turn the hearts of the fathers to the children, and the hearts of the children to their fathers, lest I come and strike the earth with a curse.*

The Elijah Task:

It is no coincidence that the Old Testament closes by saying that God would send Elijah to turn the hearts of the fathers back to the children, and vice versa, to prepare the church for Messiah. In the New Testament we are informed in Matthew 17:11-12 that many individuals who are endued with the spirit of Elijah will come to prepare the church for revival and the Second Coming of Christ.

Jesus answered and said to them, "Indeed, Elijah is coming first and will restore all things. But I say to you that Elijah has come already, and they did not know him but did to him whatever they wished. Likewise the Son of Man is also about to suffer at their hands."

What is Elijah's Task?

1. The spirit of Elijah breathes life into the next generation.[181]
2. The spirit of Elijah confronts and pulls down the ungodly structures of Baal worship in the land.[182]
3. The spirit of Elijah clears the obstacles and stumbling blocks (hurts and wounds) from God's people so they can return from captivity.[183]
4. The spirit of Elijah facilitates supernatural healing between parents and children.[184]
5. The spirit of Elijah causes people who are not obeying God to change their ways.[185]

CHAPTER FOURTEEN

The Orphan Stronghold

A Timely Word:

On September 8th, four days before our purity conference was to kick off, someone posted the following word by Chuck Pierce on Facebook:

> I am sending My presence into the dark hearts of captivity where Baals, and Ashteroths have ruled. I will cause the headship of that which has been holding My harvest fields to break, tumble and roll.
> The heads of rule are changing. I am causing My presence to de-throne that which has been ruling the thoughts of My people. In the midst of dangerous times, call for My presence to flood that which has captivated and watch the headship of the enemy fall.

Pulling Down Baal:

As noted in an earlier chapter Baal was, and continues today, to be the demonic ruler or fallen son of God that seeks to destroy families via covenant breaking (sexual perversion). On the evening of September 12th, 2014 we held our first annual purity conference. A combined total of over 750 parents and high school students gathered from 50 churches across Oahu at First Assembly of God Red Hill in Honolulu, seeking to learn how to deal with the sexual issues facing our youth. At the close of the first service 250 parents knelt before 500 youth and repented both to God and to them for having sex before marriage and sliming them with impurity. In response, the youth knelt before us and repented for their sexual sins.

Three days after the conference concluded, reports began to flow in from various sources that parents and their teens had tearfully reconciled with one another. During our Sunday worship service that same weekend, a geyser opened in the Spirit, and God's Glory filled our sanctuary. Praise and worship went to a new level, and the Lord healed two people who were dealing with painful physical issues instantaneously!

In addition to these exciting developments, lava (representing God's love?) began to flow in the lava tubes underneath Mauna Loa, Hawaii's largest active volcano. By repenting for our sexual sins and turning our hearts back to our children, and vice versa, is it possible that the Lord pulled down Baal in the heavenly realms and released revival in the Hawaiian Islands?

What is God Up to?

It is God's heart to not only heal our families (this is authentic revival), but also to bring us to maturity by equipping us for works of kingdom ministry.[186] The Greek word for 'equip' is 'Katartizo', meaning 'to mend the nets'. Katartizo is a compound word, composed of 'kata' (down) and 'artos' (a joint), and has a variety of meanings:

> *To repair, restore to a former good condition, to prepare, to fit out, to equip. It is used of reconciling factions, putting a dislocated limb into place, 'mending nets', manning a fleet, supplying an army with provisions. The basic idea is "adjustment; the putting of all the parts into right relation and connection.*[187]

A blogger, Peggy Overstreet, researched the various meanings of Katartizo and posted her findings:[188]

> In Matthew 4:21, regarding the mending of nets, the idea is that they be restored to their former condition, thus preparing them for the next day's fishing, equipping them for future service. In Luke 6:40,
> Jesus says that a pupil that "has been fully trained, will be like his teacher." Jesus' focus in discipleship is on equipping followers with character. The person who has been equipped to follow Jesus is the person who has become like Him. Paul used the verb in a meta-phorical sense of "setting a person right, of bringing him into line" in regard to maturity as a Christian. Paul says, in 1 Corinthians 1:10, instead of dividing into quarreling cliques, Christians should be "per-

fectly united in the same mind and purpose." In 2 Corinthians 13:9 and 11, Paul prays that the brethren may be "made complete." In Galatians 6:1, "restore such a one," the word refers to mending the lives of Christians, thus equipping them for usefulness in God's ser-vice. Sin caused the broken relationship, which now needs repairing, thus restoring communion with Jesus. The present tense suggests necessity for patience and perseverance in the process. In 1 Peter 5:10, "God will Himself perfect you," it speaks of rounding out the spiritual life of the saint so that he is equipped for both the living of a Christian life and the service of the Lord Jesus Christ.

What is the Orphan Stronghold?

It has always been God's intent to 'mend our nets' (we are the nets), so we can become mature sons and daughters, rule and reign, and fulfill the Great Commission.[189] The primary obstacle that blocks us from walking in sonship is the 'orphan stronghold'. The Greek word for orphan is 'orphanos' and is translated 'comfortless'. The Oxford Dictionary defines an orphan as a child whose parents are both dead,[190] while Wikipedia's definition is a child permanently bereaved or abandoned by his or her parents.[191]

Not every believer has been abandoned by one or both parents, nor has every believer been parented the way God originally intended, leaving them comfortless in some way. In his book, Experiencing The Father's Embrace, Jack Frost lists six different 'father types': the Absent Dad; the Abusive Dad; the Authoritarian Dad; the Passive Dad; the Performance Oriented Dad and the Good Dad. Frost's description of each of these father types, which also ap-plies to mothers, explains how we are emotionally wounded or made comfort-less by our parents' imperfections.

Whether intentionally or unintentionally, our parents have wounded us creat-ing 'comfortlessness' within our souls, and this is the orphan stronghold. A stronghold is something that has a 'strong hold' on you. If we are to walk in the sonship that God has reserved for us before the foundation of the world, God must heal our hearts and fill us with the experiential knowledge of His perfect love through the Comforter.

We Are God's Pleasure!

The greatest struggle that most of us seem to have is embracing our identity in Christ. We recall that when Jesus was baptized in the Jordan River,[192] the heavens opened over Him and the Father lovingly whispered, "This is my Son in whom I am well-pleased." Three observations:

1. The Father blessed Jesus before He performed a single miracle, meaning that His love for Jesus was not predicated on His performance but upon His person. Translation: The Father loved the Son for who He was, not for what He could do.

2. The Father released His pleasure upon Jesus. The Greek word for pleased is 'eudokeo', meaning to think well; approve; consent or take delight.[193] The Son knew His Father's love and approval experientially, not just conceptually. The Bible tells us that David, a type of son or Jesus, experienced the tangible pleasure of God: You make known to me the path of life; in your presence there is fullness of joy; at your right hand are pleasures forevermore.[194]

3. The Father sent the Comforter to comfort Jesus because of the challenges that Jesus would face as the Second Adam. Although Jesus was 100 percent God He was also fully human. The Comforter, or Holy Spirit, is the Spirit of Abba.[195] When we receive Jesus into our hearts we become His children, and the Comforter is downloaded into our hearts to assure us that the Father carries us in His heart. This is the baptism of the Spirit.

Orphan Struggles:

Many of us do not have the revelation that God carries us in His heart and that we are blessed with every blessing in Christ.[196] Because of both the Fall and imperfect parenting, we each struggle with a wide spectrum of strongholds that hinder us from becoming mature in Christ and from accessing the divine privileges of sonship—discernment and wisdom.[197]

There are 12 issues that orphan believers typically struggle with:

1. Mistrust of Authority
2. Abandonment
3. Belonging
4. Insecurity
5. Fear of rejection
6. Poverty thinking
7. Giving and receiving love
8. Religious mindsets
9. Performing and striving
10. Relating honestly
11. Overcoming trials and challenges

12. Divine identity

The above orphan structures of mind and heart contend with our ability to see ourselves the way God sees us, and to accept who He says we are. God has called us to function as sons and daughters (and kings and queens). He has given us permission to steward His power and divine resources for the benefit of others. May we rule and reign as sons and daughters and kings and queens!

Orphanage to Family:

Presently, the Lord is transitioning and transforming the body of Christ from a global orphanage into a worldwide family. From the 1980's through the end of the 20th century there was reawakening within the body of Christ to the person and presence of the Holy Sprit, spiritual gifts, etc. At the turn of the 21st century, the revelation of the Father and His unquenchable love for His sons and daughters began to trickle into the church in order to deal with the orphan stronghold. Recently, it has become clear that God has been working overtime to convince us that we are who He says we are in His Word.

You Have Not Many Fathers:

Most of us struggle with our identity in Christ because we were not mentored or 'poured into' by our fathers. The apostle Paul wrote in 1 Corinthians 4:14-17:

> *I do not write these things to shame you, but as my beloved children I warn you. For though you might have ten thousand instructors in Christ, yet you do not have many fathers; for in Christ Jesus I have begotten you through the gospel. Therefore I urge you, imitate me. For this reason I have sent Timothy to you, who is my beloved and faithful son in the Lord, who will remind you of my ways in Christ, as I teach everywhere in every church.*

It is time for the fathers (and mothers) to arise! This will take time. Many spiritual fathers and mothers are presently being raised up by God to help transition the church into a family. Parenting is a high call. Contrary to the saying that it takes an entire village to raise a child, I think it takes a healthy church to train and equip parents so they can raise healthy sons and daughters.

Few dads understand their call, let alone their divine job description. Derek Prince identifies three specific functions of fatherhood: priest, prophet, and king or ruler. [198]

Priest—The primary function of the Old Testament priests was to intercede and declare blessings on behalf of the nation of Israel. When Israel was exiled to Babylon, they no longer had access to the temple in Jerusalem so their homes became mini-sanctuaries or house temples, and each father was considered the priest of his home, and the dinner table became the family altar.[199] Fathers are called by God to pray for their families, to intercede for their wives and children.

Prophet—In the Old Testament, prophets were known for delivering the word of the Lord to the people of God. Sometimes it would be a spoken utterance and at other times it would be acted out prophetically.[200] What is the primary prophetic message that the Father wants fathers to act out, or demonstrate, before their children? He wants them to reveal His loving nature through their everyday interactions with their children. Of course, on this side of heaven, we cannot perfectly reveal the Father's love, but by doing our best to love our children unconditionally through our actions and words they can taste and see that the Father is love.

King or Ruler—Fathers are also called by God to lead their homes. Their call is not only to provide financially for their families, but also to lead their wives and children in the pursuit of God and the application of His word.

Keys For Breaking Free From The Orphan Stronghold:

In order to transition us from orphanage to family, God has been doing more than raising up fathers. He has also been teaching us how to break free from the orphan stronghold. Listed below are 10 keys:

1. Recognize, get the revelation, that you have orphan issues (areas of comfortlessness in your heart).
2. Reflect on the feedback you have received from your spouse, loved ones or circle of friends; and ask yourself:
   a. Have I rebelled against or dishonored my parents in any way?
   b. Do I have any unresolved anger or bitterness in my heart towards my parents?
3. Take personal responsibility for your attitudes and actions by asking your parents to forgive you for any ungodly attitudes or actions towards them.
4. Ask your parents to bless you.
5. If your parents have passed away or are not willing or capable of blessing you, ask a spiritual mother or father to bless you in their place.

6. Go to your children and ask them to forgive you for any way that you have hurt, abandoned or neglected them.
7. Bless your children.
8. Spend time daily with your children (listening, laughing, blessing, mentoring etc.).
9. Pray the Prayer of Restitution (Chapter 16).
10. Decree and declare that you are God's beloved son or daughter, His king or queen.

CHAPTER FIFTEEN

Melchizedek and the Gift of Discernment

In the spring of 2010, I began feeling that we should gather together at the beginning of Pentecost, the evening of May 22 at sundown; so I invited who-ever wanted to come and join me at Aslan's Place. I arrived at 7:30pm and a small group assembled as sundown approached. As we waited, we could feel the presence of the Lord increasing and, as the sunlight disappeared, we felt a slight breeze moving through the room. At 7:50pm, the anointing rapidly increased and we felt we were to stand and join hands; but then, all of a sudden, I started running backwards. Now, I want to tell you that I have not even run forward in a long time!

I ran backwards around the living room at a full run seven times. On the final return to my chair, the Lord sat me down and I asked, "Okay, what was that all about?" Each person had a different idea. One said I was unwinding; another said I was undoing; and another said I was going backwards to something. I was mystified, and wondered for many weeks what this meant.

Also during the spring of 2010, the discernment of something new began. I was on the phone with Rob Gross and together we realized that I was discerning Melchizedek. As I pondered what it meant to discern Melchizedek,

I kept saying to others and especially to Rob, "I do not get this." I listened to a set of tapes and read a couple of books about Melchizedek but still was not satisfied—I knew that there was something more the Lord wanted me to understand. This was a mystery that I was supposed to comprehend, but what was it?

In searching out the things of God I often say I need my 'ah-ha'—the moment of clarity when all that the Lord is trying to communicate finally makes sense. My ah-ha moment in regard to Melchizedek finally came when the Lord reminded of the very beginning of my training to discern good and evil; and I remembered that He had given me Hebrews 5:14 just after I had conducted my first seminar on discernment, Discerning the Battle, in Virginia. I had returned home when my friend, Dr. Tom Hawkins, called and said "The Lord gave me a verse for you," and Hebrews 5:14 became the foundational verse for God's call on my life to teach discernment.

> But solid food belongs to those who are of full age, that is, those who by reason of use have their senses exercised to discern both good and evil.

Now, years later, my ah-ha moment occurred when I finally realized that this verse is right in the middle of the passage about Melchizedek.

After twenty years, the Lord had brought me back to the beginning days and showed me that discernment is really all about recognizing the intercession of Melchizedek. It's about knowing what the Lord Jesus is interceding for in his function as the eternal high priest, Melchizedek, and then doing what the Father is doing. All these years I had been in training, learning to discern many different kinds of spiritual beings; angels, seraphim, cherubim, elders, rulers, elemental spirits, orbs, powers, etc. Now I knew that the purpose of my training had not been just to recognize these beings, but also to understand Melchizedek's intercession before the Father as the High Priest. By discerning the spiritual being(s) present I would be able to see what the Father was doing because He has trained me in regard to their purposes and functions, and I would know how to respond based on my discernment. I would understand how to do what the Father is doing.

For years I was told that discernment (the use of the physical senses to know what is going on in the spiritual realm) is unnecessary and is, indeed, unbiblical. I now understand that not only is discernment necessary, but it is also essential to entering into and understanding the new realms that God has for us.

Now, about four years later, I understand something new about the revelation of Melchizedek, who is first revealed when Abram gained victory over the descendants of the fallen sons of God. Who is Melchizedek?

Genesis 14 tells of nine kings and nations that were warring. Abram became involved in the conflict because Lot, his brother's son, had been taken prisoner. Along with 318 servants, he pursued these enemies, attacking them and rescuing Lot. After Abram's return from the battle, Melchizedek suddenly appeared before him. Then Melchizedek, King of Salem, brought out bread and wine and, acting as the priest of God Most High, he pronounced a blessing:

> "Blessed be Abram of God Most High, Possessor of heaven and earth; and blessed be God Most High, who has delivered your enemies into your hand." And he gave him a tithe of all.[201]

I believe that Melchizedek is the eternal High Priest, who later came as Je-sus Christ. Melchizedek is the function of Jesus Christ as THE eternal High Priest, always interceding for us. As mentioned in scripture, Melchizedek is the King of Peace (Salem) as well as the King of Righteousness.

Melchizedek blessed Abram because the Lord had delivered the enemies of Abram into his hands. I wondered, could it be that when we are aware of Melchizedek, it is an indication that He is giving us victory over our enemies? I realized that this is what I had been asking the Lord for when, some months before, I had been sitting in the Jacuzzi, worn out because I had been battling witchcraft and I prayed, "Lord, when do we ever win?"

A righteous anger came up inside me saying, "How dare these people exercise witchcraft and come against the God Most High?"

I got really angry and asked again, "God, when do we ever win? Lord, why don't you display your glory and remove those who come against Your Kingdom plans?" I prayed for grace and mercy for them but also declared, "Oh God arise and destroy your enemies."

Isn't it time for God's vengeance against his enemies? Isn't it time for the Kingdom of God to advance? The revelation of Melchizedek would seem to indicate that we are now moving into a period of time in which we will have victory over our enemies. The Lord prophetically showed this to me one day.

Song lyrics were running through my head all day, "I'm going down to the riverside, riverside, riverside and I'm not going to study war anymore." I thought, "OK I'll get it." That evening I went to watch the new Chronicles of Narnia film, Prince Caspian. The movie seemed to be a flow of constant battling, the children having now forgotten much about Aslan were determined that they could win the war against the enemy. They were convinced that Aslan, the type of Christ, was not necessary and they could win the war without Him.

Finally Lucy said, "I'm going to go find Aslan for help," and Peter realized the battle was over and he'd lost. Then the enemy said, "Let's go down to the riverside to finish this battle." But when they went there, Aslan showed up and the battle was over. In the last scene of the movie, the enemy was laying their swords and shields down by the riverside. I pondered this for some time, and came to realize that the revelation of Melchizedek is the fulfillment of that prophetic scene. Melchizedek is revealed when we can finally enter into His rest, allowing Him to bring victory over our enemies.

Melchizedek is a king and a priest, and He belongs to the Order of Melchizedek. Our Heavenly Father has always wanted His people to be an order of kings and priests. In fact, that was His intention for the Children of Israel but they did not want it, and the people refused the position. It was then that the Lord set aside the tribe of Levi to act as priests for the people. But, after the resurrection of Jesus Christ, the Church entered into a new position. Believers are declared to be a royal priesthood—we are now kingly priests and belong to the order of Melchizedek.

As noted above, we first see Melchizedek in Genesis 14. Just before that chapter, we see that Abraham had been called to the Promised Land by God, but Lot had decided to stay on the east side of the Jordan River. Genesis 14 begins with a list of four kings who are warring against five other kings.[202] One might easily skip over this section, but a close examination of these kings will reveal a strong connection to the fallen sons of God. Let's look at these kings.

1. **Amraphel, King of Shinar**—Shinar is probably identical to Babylonia or Southern Mesopotamia, and Amraphel may be Nimrod,[203] who was said to be a mighty[204] one on the earth

2. **Arioch, King of Ellasar**—Ellasar may have been located in southern Babylon, and Arioch means 'servant of the moon god'.[205] He may have been the grandson of Nimrod[206]

3. **Chedorlaomer, King of Elam**—His name means 'servant of Lagamar', a goddess in the Elamite pantheon[207]

4. **Tidal, King of nations**—Perhaps he has a Hittite connection[208]

5. **Bera, King of Sodom**—Bera means son of evil[209]

6. **Birsha, King of Gomorrah**—Birsha means sons of wickedness[210]
7. **Shinab, King of Admah**—Tied to the moon god, meaning 'sin is my father'[211]
8. **Shemeber, King of Zeboiim**--Meaning 'lofty flight'[212]
9. **King of Bela (that is, Zoar)**—Bela means destruction[213]

In the fourteenth year Chedorlaomer and the kings that were with him came and attacked the Rephaim in Ashtoreth Karnaim, the Zuzim in Ham, the Emim in Shaveh Kiriathaim.[214]

The Rephaim were tied to the giants, the Nephilim that are mentioned in Genesis 6.[215] Ashtoreth is the Canaanite fertility goddess tied to Baal.[216] Zuzim means 'roving creatures'[217] who were inhabitants of Ammon, a place where the giants dwelled.[218] Emim means 'terror'.[219]

Seen throughout this chapter is the warring of those who appear to be descendants of the Nephilim. As we've seen above, it was after Lot was captured and Abram rescued him that Melchizedek appeared, brought out bread and wine, and blessed him.

Melchizedek, meaning King of Righteousness, is also the King of Peace.[220] Melchizedek is therefore both a priest and a king, and he gave a blessing to Abram because he had victory over his enemies, which I believe is essential to our understanding of Melchizedek. Note that the blessing came because Abram's victory was over the fallen sons of God. The victory over our enemies is also mentioned in both the Psalms and in the Hebrews passages about Melchizedek.

After the brief account of Melchizedek in Genesis, there is no more mention of Him until 900 years later during the time of King David. It is noteworthy that although David was a king, he also once went into the holy place and ate of the table of showbread, therefore acting like a kingly priest. David clearly stated in Psalm 110 that Melchizedek is tied to victory over one's enemies.

The Lord said to my Lord, "Sit at My right hand, till I make Your enemies Your footstool." The Lord shall send the rod of your strength out of Zion. Rule in the midst of Your enemies! The Lord has sworn and will not relent, "You are a priest forever according to the order of Melchizedek." [221]

Now, fast-forward through over 900 additional years until hearing of Melchizedek again. The New Testament book of Hebrews offers the most detailed description of Melchizedek and speaks clearly about the function of Jesus Christ as High Priest. In Hebrews 5-8, we are reminded that Jesus is forever Melchizedek. He is the King of Peace and the King of Righteousness. It is this wonderful Jesus, the Perfect One; who, because of His intercession, enables us to endure and have hope in the future. This Melchizedek is not a priest of the tribe of Levi, but of the tribe of Judah. The entire passage crescendos in Hebrews 8:1-2:

> *Now this is the main point of the things we are saying: we have such a High Priest, who is seated at the right hand of the throne of the Majesty in the heavens, a Minister of the sanctuary and of the true tabernacle which the Lord erected, and not man.*

If there is still any doubt that Jesus is Melchizedek, His own words, should be noted:

> *"Your father Abraham rejoiced to see My day, and he saw it and was glad."*[222]

When could Abraham have seen Jesus? Only when He appeared to him as Melchizedek, as recorded in Genesis 14.

But how do we really comprehend Melchizedek? This knowing is not just an 'intellectual knowing', but is a 'discernment knowing'; a knowing that arises through the five physical senses. Melchizedek is difficult to comprehend without physical discernment.

CHAPTER SIXTEEN

Melchizedek's War

When I ran backwards on Passover I really had come full circle, returning to the beginnings of my discernment and the beginnings of my warfare. However, I had returned to the beginning with a richer understanding. Warfare is about warring against the fallen sons of God who are the real enemies of the Lord, and we have come into the crosshairs of that war. We have been drafted into this battle when we gave our lives to the Lord, and His enemies have now become our enemies. We are at a distinct disadvantage and this battle is impossible to fight on our own. There is good news though—the battle is not ours, but the Lord's, and He has won the victory through His death on the cross. But we must still do our part.

Gregory Boyd has written clearly about this.

Thus, the Christian life is for Paul a life of spiritual military service. It is about being a good soldier (2 Tim 2:4), about "fighting the good fight" (1 Tim 1:18; 6:12), about "waging war" (2 Cor 10:3), and about "struggling" with a cosmic enemy (Eph. 6:12).

Given his view of the ever-present reality of Satan and his kingdom, and given his understanding of what Christ was about and what the church is supposed to be about, it is hard to see how [Paul] could have viewed the Christian life differently."[223]

We are entering a new season in which we begin to understand how to participate in this war. We are learning new weapons of warfare, and now understand that we are to war from a state of rest. We realize that we need to fine-tune our five physical senses so we are aware of the intercession of Melchizedek for when we have done that, we are able to know what the response of the Father is to Jesus' intercession and respond accordingly.

One day the words of Daniel 7:26-27 will be fulfilled and we, as the revealed sons of God, will fully rule and reign with Jesus Christ who is the victorious and totally unique and only begotten Son of God.

> *But the court shall be seated, and they shall take away his [the enemy's] domin-ion, to consume and destroy it forever. Then the kingdom and dominion, and the greatness of the kingdoms under the whole heaven, shall be given to the people, the saints of the Most High. His kingdom is an everlasting kingdom, and all dominions shall serve and obey Him.*

CHAPTER SEVENTEEN

Prayer of Restitution

Lord, I renounce and repent for those in my family line who broke marriage covenants and mated with the fallen sons of God.

I also renounce and repent for all Moloch and Baal worship in my generational line. On behalf of both sides of the family, please forgive us for choosing to fashion the golden calf at the foot of Mount Sinai when we were too afraid to draw near to You because we feared Your might and power. Forgive us for not waiting for the return of Your servant, Moses, and for breaking covenant with You by worshiping the golden calf through sacrificial burnt and peace offerings.

Forgive us for holding a festival to the golden calf and indulging ourselves in pagan revelry and sexual sin. Most of all Lord, I renounce and repent for first believing, and then declaring, "These are your gods, O Israel, who brought you out of Egypt"; when it was You who set us free from 430 years of Egyptian captivity. Lord, please forgive us for this wanton display of pride, self-deception, stubbornness and unbelief.

Forgive us Father, for not only worshiping the golden calf and sacrificing our children to it, but also for worshiping the star god Rephan, or Saturn, while wandering in the wilderness for 40 years.

On behalf of every ancestor in my family line who entered the land of Canaan after wandering 40 years in the wilderness, I renounce and repent for our refusal to obey Your explicit command not to engage in the pagan sexual practices of incest, adultery, homosexuality and bestiality that were intertwined with the worship of Moloch. Forgive us for sacrificing our sons and daughters in the fires of Moloch in exchange for favor and prosperity. I know this idolatry was a great offense to You, and I now repent and apologize.

On behalf of every ancestor who was involved with Baal or Moloch worship throughout the history of Israel; from the generation who succeeded Joshua, to the reign of Jeroboam, to Ahab and Jezebel, to Manasseh and beyond; I renounce and repent for every evil connected to this false lord-ruler including child sacrifice, sorcery, witchcraft and the worship of the stars of heaven.

Lord, I now ask You to open every bronze door that has been shut in my generational line because of Baal and Moloch worship so that the righteous gates the enemy has closed and contaminated can no longer be shut. Come now King of Glory, flood the heavenly places in my generational line with Your cleansing power and unseal what the enemy has sealed in the heavenly places, making straight every crooked path and smoothing out every rough place. Smash the bronze doors Lord, and sever the iron bars of my captivity. I now declare that what You have opened will remain open and what You have shut will remain shut. Prepare the way of the Lord.

Lord, I repent for and renounce all worship of the rulers of darkness in my town, city and state. I ask you to forgive me, my family line and the citizens of this region for worshiping false gods at false altars, sacrificing our children to Moloch, and breaking the covenant of marriage through incest, adultery, homosexuality and bestiality. On behalf of the church, I repent for not fearing Your name, not obeying Your Word, not obeying the leading of Your Spirit; and for presuming upon your grace that we can sin sexually, defy spiritual authority, and not suffer the consequences. Please forgive us for slandering the glorious ones and disconnecting ourselves from Your Glory.

Lord, please disconnect me from the ungodly Mazzaroth and cleanse my spirit, soul and body down to the cellular and sub cellular levels from all ungodly influence, defilement and power.

Please remove all parts of my trifold being from the lowest regions of the ungodly depths by disconnecting me from the Nephilim and Rephaim and removing any witchcraft bands from around my arms.

Please transfer me from Mount Horeb to Mount Zion and reconnect me back to the glorious ones so Your light will shine through me to others as I proclaim the Gospel in power to Jerusalem, Samaria and to the ends of the earth.

Please disconnect me from the mountains of Esau and move me to Mt. Zion.

I declare to my spirit that you will be under and submissive to the Holy Spirit; and I declare to my body and soul that you will be submissive to my spirit, even as my spirit is submissive to the Holy Spirit.

Lord, please balance correctly the male and female portions of my human spirit.

Please remove all fractal imaging in my family line and remove all mirrors. I declare I will only reflect the image and nature of the Lord Jesus Christ.

Please remove me from the ungodly council and establish me on Mt. Zion and in your heavenly council.

Lord, I repent for those in my family line who turned our family line over to the enemy, thus giving authority for the removal of righteous elders and permission for establishing unrighteous elders over us. I acknowledge that these unrighteous elders caused the family to veer off course, moving out of the right time sequence into other time sequences. I now declare, as a revealed son of God, that these unrighteous elders must leave my family line. Father, please establish the righteous elders over my family line and put us back on the right course and into the right time, removing us from Chronos time and placing us into Your Kairos time.

On behalf of the entire church, forgive me Lord, for syncing my life according to Chronos time and my plans and agendas, instead of Your Kairos time and agenda. Please forgive me Lord for not inquiring of You to see what You want, where You are moving and what You are doing.

Forgive me for believing the lie that Your Second Coming is so close that I need not reach out to the lost and fulfill Your Great Commission. I decree and declare Lord, that it is time to align my life with Yours.

Please remove me from Chronos time and sync me with Kairos time. Open every bronze door so that the gates are no longer shut. Open all the righteous doors and flood my life with Your Glory.
Please remove me from any ungodly place in the depth where parts of me are trapped by sonar, and release your righteous sound that will neutralize that ungodly sonar. Please free all of my trapped parts and fragments.

Please break all ungodly ties and connections between myself and the Rephaim or any other person's soul parts, and remove those connectors.

I renounce and repent for those in my family line who traded their souls for favors from the enemy. Please, through the Blood of Jesus, return all scattered soul parts back to my family line and me. I command Beelzebub to leave.

I ask, Lord Jesus, that you will come as the Son of Man and remove all fallen sons of God from my family line and me.

Please disconnect me from Abaddon and remove any parts of me from the bottomless pit.

Please unlock the ciphers and the ungodly algorithms established by the enemy.

I renounce and repent for those in my family line who gave over the family line to the enemy in order to be able to rule and control others for their own advantage and financial gain. I now understand that this gave the enemy the right to cause me to be knit in the ungodly depth; placing me in a position of servitude rather than one of ruling and reigning over creation, which is my God given right. Please take me back in time to the origin, to your womb of the dawn, and please knit me together in the Godly depth. Please remove from me all DNA and RNA contamination that took place during the ungodly knitting.

I declare that I will not be in subjection to others by means of their control and abuse. Lord, please remove the desolation of generations and take me out of any ungodly places in the depth or the height, disconnecting me from those regions and placing me in the Godly depth and in the Godly height. I reject the discord that has imprisoned me because of my agreement with the ungodly position in which I found myself. I repent for believing the lie that I was to be in submission to others without having any voice, and that this position was normal and was ordained by God.

Please release the righteous sound and vibrations that will align me with the heavenly sounds and vibrations.

Please disconnect me from the dark angels and other unrighteous beings that rule in the ungodly height.

I recognize that my mindset of being a victim has inhibited my ability to fulfill the call on my life to rule and reign under the Lordship of Jesus Christ. I also declare that the wealth that I am to gain for the purposes of the Kingdom of God has been stopped up by my ancestors' sin of wanting personal wealth to use for their own purposes. I now declare that I will receive all the wealth that the Lord wants me to have to fulfill my Kingdom mandate of ruling and reigning. Lord, please release all restrictions against the resources that you originally intended for me to have.

I declare that I will rule and reign in the Godly height under the Lordship of Jesus Christ, and I will use all created resources for His Kingdom.

I renounce and repent for my family line and myself for all who entered into sexual activity outside of marriage. Please break the consequences of those who were molested and became victims of sexual abuse. I also repent for all of us who have used pornography for sexual satisfaction. I understand that all this sexual activity resulted in our joining to someone other than our spouses.

Lord, as an adult, I ask that You remove me from my parent's sphere of influence and place me in my own sphere of influence. Please remove me from the ungodly length and place me into your Godly length.

Father, I come in the name of your Son, Jesus; Your only begotten Son; the only Son of God who became a son of man who takes His place upon us, His body. I come into agreement with a common passion to see heaven's intention that was built and established before the foundation of the earth. I ask you, Heavenly Father, Righteous Judge of heaven and earth, to issue a decree against the fallen sons. I call our bloodlines back. Please remove us from the ungodly womb of the dawn. I take back our households in the name of Jesus of Nazareth. I surrender them through the blood of Jesus Christ to be sanctified, glorified, and to come into alignment with their place in the kingdom of Melchizedek. I will no longer drink the wine of the fallen sons of God. I renounce and denounce the spirit of religion, the spirit of debate, the spirit of legalism, the spirit of opinion, the spirit of criticism and the spirit of high-minded intellect. I renounce the mind of the old Adamic way, as well as any mindsets that have been born of the doctrines of the fallen sons of man and the fallen sons of God. I ask for a divorce decree between the fallen sons of God and us. I choose to no longer put faith in the defeated enemy but in the victorious Son of God, Jesus Christ.

Lord, I ask you to reverse the polarity of any ungodly device and extract us from the ungodly collective; removing all microchips, transmitters, and receivers. Extract from my mind all voices and communication from others. Re-move me from the ungodly width and the ungodly cloud. I choose to no longer to be affected by the ungodly thoughts of others.

Please destroy all molecules, atomic, and sub atomic particles created by the fallen sons of God.

Please destroy any dimensions, kingdoms or spheres that the fallen sons of

God created due to the agreement of my ancestors or myself.

On behalf of my family line I repent for all blood that was shed on the land and for all idolatry and sexual sin committed on any land area. Please break all ungodly ties between my ancestors and myself with any land area.

Please remove ungodly words of the fallen sons of God that were added to my original design when I was knit together in the deep.

Please activate any righteous words that were covered up by the fallen sons of God on my scroll when I was knit together in the deep.

Please remove any mismatch and misaligning that took place when I was knit together in the deep; remove all ungodly elders, rulers and powers that were involved when I was knit together in the deep; and remove all stones from the fallen sons of God that were knit into me in the deep.

Please break all ungodly agreement between the ungodly deep and the ungodly height, and disconnect me from all fallen stars, star systems, galaxies, and constellations that were involved in contaminating my original design.

Please remove off of me all contamination from the fallen sons of God that affected the light, sound, frequencies, vibrations and colors that made up my being.

Please remove any genes added by the fallen sons of God. Please repair any genes damaged by the fallen sons of God and return to my DNA any genes that were taken away by the fallen sons of God.

Please destroy any ungodly cloning of my genes and chromosomes. Please undo any ungodly fusion with evil that took place with me.

Lord, I ask that You will come with your measuring rod and linen cord and measure the temple in me, removing all generational ungodly temples, kingdoms, spheres, doors, gates, altars, pillars, priestly garments, worship tools and sacrifices.

[Women] Lord Jesus, I understand that as a child I may have accepted the lie that a female was not to become more than a male would permit. I under-stand that this may have crushed my spirit and caused parts of my spirit to be trapped in the ungodly width. I now reject that lie and I declare that I will be all that the Lord Jesus has created me to be. Please remove all parts of my spirit that have been trapped in the ungodly width and in the ungodly stars, star systems, constellations and zodiacs. I no longer allow the enemy to project around me that I am worthless and that I am always a victim and powerless. I will take my position in Christ and rule and reign equally with males. Please disconnect me from all fallen sons of God who have perpetuated this lie in my family line.

Father, I recognize that the fallen sons of God did not want to be your sons, and so disconnected themselves from you as Father and established themselves as father. I also acknowledge that this may have resulted in generational parts and parts of me to have been trapped in Saturn, the fallen stars, star systems, ungodly galaxies, constellations and zodiacs and in the ungodly length, width, height, and depth.

I renounce and repent for those in my family line who did the same thing with their fathers, and were so distraught about their fathers that they disconnected themselves from them and declared that they would be fathers without being a child. I understand that this established a disconnection generationally between father and child, resulting in generational blessings not being passed down the family line. I also acknowledge that this may have prohibited me from taking my place as a revealed son of God. I acknowledge that this ungodly fractal pattern may have caused a disconnection between father and child resulting in bitterness and anger in my family line and in my life. I now ask, Lord, that You would remove me from Saturn, the fallen stars, star systems, ungodly galaxies, constellations and zodiacs and in the ungodly length, width, height, and depth.

I now forgive my father and all fathers in my family line for not fathering correctly. I also forgive all sons and daughters in my family line that, because of the cruelty of their fathers, disconnected themselves from their fathers and broke the God-intended linkage between generations, thus also breaking the free flow of generational blessings.

Lord, please connect my generational line and me correctly to the Godly length, width, height and depth so that I can take my place as a revealed son of God and rule and reign with Christ. I also ask that You will correctly connect me to my generational line so that the generational blessings that were to come down the family line will now be completely restored to the family line and to myself. I reclaim and receive your spiritual blessings that were intended for my family line and me. I now ask that what has happened in the heavenly places will now be done on earth in the physical realm. I now claim all physical, emotional, and spiritual health that you intend me to have. I also claim all physical inheritance that is my right as a revealed son of God.

Lord Jesus, by your life sacrificed on the cross and by your life-blood, please dismantle and remove all structures that have been built from these sins and from unclean spirits, including ungodly habits, curses, devices, conduits, attachments, lies, "gifts" or deposits. Free us from ungodly structures, from distortions in my life and family line, and even from any distortions of our DNA and RNA. God Almighty, please close any doors or openings that these sins and ungodly structures created. Open any Godly doors to you and your blessings that these sins and ungodly structures had closed. Holy Spirit, please empower righteous choices in my family line and myself. I choose to honor You, growing Godly habits while enthroning Your name in our lives, relation-ships, and land.

CHAPTER EIGHTEEN

Ruling and Reigning With Christ Prayer

Lord Jesus, I repent for any decision that I may have made with the enemy before conception because of fear or doubt about your goodness and your plan for my life. I understand that this decision may have resulted in the right for the enemy to negatively affect my DNA and RNA and the living water that was to flow out of me. I now exercise my authority in Christ, based on the finished work of the cross and the blood of Christ, over the contamination of the fiery stones and the living water. I now ask you, Lord, to remove the influence of wormwood over the living water and purify that water. Please remove me from any ungodly orbs, trapezoids, and geospheres in all dimensions and from the ungodly depth.

Please release into me the fullness of your living water and assign to me all righteous lights. I now ask that You will come against all assignments made against me and heal all of my diseases.

Please remove from me any ungodly coating and all ungodly garments.

Please remove me from any ungodly constellations and all ungodly zodiacs.

Please close all ungodly gates and doors that give the enemy access to me, especially through any ungodly triangles, tetrahedrons, and trapezoids.

Please purify all the living water assigned to me.

Please remove all ungodly water spirits and seducing spirits.

I repent and renounce for all ungodly baptisms and water rituals. Please remove me from Wormwood and from all ungodly places in the depth, height, length, and width associated with wormwood.

Please disconnect me from all ungodly stars.

Please reconnect me according to your original design to the depth, height, length, and width; and bring all Godly dimensions and quadrants into perfect equality.

I repent for all generation bestiality. Please bring all uncontaminated fiery stones back to me through Your blood.

Lord please remove all animal, fish, bird, and Nephilim DNA and RNA from my DNA and RNA. Please remove all reptilian scales from my eyes and the seven spiritual eyes you have given to me.

In the name of Jesus Christ, I repent for anytime I may have said that I did not want You to make me or that I was angry about how You made me, and I decided that I would remake myself. I repent for any time I was unwilling to yield to You as the clay yields to the potter. I repent for any time I chose the enemy's plan rather than Your plan.

I understand that any decisions I made before conception may have given the enemy a right to take the jewels of my spirit into the void and the darkness. I also understand that this may have affected my spiritual authority and my ability to rule and reign, and may have also sealed up the treasures in darkness that you intend me to have.

I acknowledge that in my generational line this may have resulted in phallic worship and the lust of the eyes, declaring that we would produce our own seed without you, and that we would save ourselves through prostitutional idolatry, trying to reproduce without You, Lord.

I acknowledge that my generational line and I may have tried to multiply and fill the earth without You, Lord, by trying to find secret knowledge. I repent for discontentment with Your ways, Your design of Me, how You made me, what You gave to me, and the authority, position, and place you have assigned to me.

I acknowledge that this may have affected the spiritual eyes that You have given me, and may have resulted in all kinds of barrenness.

I ask that You will return to me through Your blood any parts of my spirit that may be scattered in the void. Lord, please resurrect all parts of my spirit.

I now declare that I will rule and reign with the scepter that You have given to me. Lord, please correctly align the scepter You have given to me with the stone in my hand and the seven eyes of the Lamb.

I now repent for trying to be my own sacrifice, rather than acknowledging that you are the only sacrifice. I remove myself from the ungodly altar and I declare that I am seated with Christ in heavenly places and that I will rule and reign with My God. Lord, please remove any dragons from me that are seated on any thrones.

Lord Jesus, I take my position as a revealed son of God and I stand against the spirit of Shebna who has taken the key of David in my family line and restricted the access that You desire me to have to the house of wisdom and the Godly height. I acknowledge that this spirit has hewn a grave, placed him-self in the ungodly height and the ungodly rock, perverting the Rock, who is Jesus. I now ask that You will throw this one, who is the leader of the ungodly mighty men, away violently. Please seize him, turn violently against him, and toss him like a ball into a large country where he will die with all of his ungodly chariots. Please cause him to bring shame to his master's house and drive him out of his office and position so that he will be pulled down. I do not allow the spirit of Shebna to cause me to dwell in his ungodly tabernacle.

I now ask Lord Jesus, that You will take key of David and place it on Your shoulder, and I declare that You are the rightful authority over the Father's house because the Father has delegated the house to You. I acknowledge that You are clothed with a robe, You are strengthened with a belt, and all in my household is now Your responsibility.

Lord, I now declare that you are in the role of Eliakim, You are fastened in a secure place, and You occupy a glorious throne in Your Father's house. I acknowledge that all of the glory of Your Father's house is hung on You and on all Your sons and daughters. I declare that Your glory now fills all the vessels from the smallest to the greatest.

Please remove Shebna's peg and the burden that was on it. I cut it off because the Lord has spoken.

I declare that all the gates and doors that Jesus opens will remain open and all the gates and doors that Jesus closes will remain closed. I declare that my family and I will no longer be contained by the religious system and false houses; that my tent pegs will be extended and I will operate in the sphere of authority that the Lord has given to me; and I will no longer be contained by mere men. I break the power of all words of containment off of me, as well as all words of jealousy and envy and gossip. Lord, shut these ungodly gates and doors that encircle me, and open up the righteous gates and doors that You are knocking on to give me the ability to come and go as the Holy Spirit directs.

I break off the power of limitations, of pastors' and leaders words, and of the ungodly words of the body of Christ.

I declare that Jesus will be my God, and I will be His person.

I choose to submit myself unto others, even as they submit themselves unto me.

I declare that the Body of Christ and I will now make up the one new man in Christ, in which every joint will supply and everyone will do his part.

I am no longer the audience. I am the participant. Lord, you will remove the ungodly rock, for I declare that the Lord Jesus Christ is my Rock; and He will destroy the systems of the world and fill the Earth as a great mountain.

CHAPTER NINETEEN

Introduction to the Prayer to Establish Us as Kings and Priests

On Tuesday, February 28, 2012, a friend (who gave me a gift of a key lock and two keys) came in with a client. During our time together, I discerned a large orb in my left hand, and noticed that the outside of the orb felt good but the inside was evil. My sense was that the orb was the sphere of influence that I was to have as a Christian. The inside of the orb was made up of stars, star systems, and dimensions, but they felt contaminated. I also felt two gates on the orb. Then I noticed that both my friend and the client also had an orb in their left hands.

During the all-day ministry session, the Lord gave us understanding about what to pray in order to clean our orbs. We developed a prayer throughout the day and then prayed it together; after which, I felt the orb was clean.

We came to understand that kingdoms and governments are tied to the stars. When we are rightly aligned to the Kingdom of God, we can then rule and reign under Christ in the spheres of influence that He has for us.

During the time of ministry, my son Brian was erasing and reinstalling the hard drive of my computer. I felt this was prophetic. It was as if the Lord was erasing all the ungodly codes and regulations that had been built up in our DNA and RNA through multiple generations of sin.

I noticed that after we prayed I experienced deliverance throughout Tuesday night and all day on Wednesday. It was not until the evening that it stopped. Then, after our youth group on Thursday, I realized that the Lord was doing deliverance on those who were there as well. I also noticed that something dramatic had happened, and there was a distinct change in the way I was feeling deliverance. Before I had felt the deliverance on a certain part of my head, but it was now going through the spiritual scepter I felt on my left hand and also through the spiritual elder's rod on my front left hand side. Since then, I continue to feel deliverances taking place there. I also have a lessened sense of evil, unless I am praying for people.

CHAPTER TWENTY

Prayer to Establish us as Kings and Priests in His Kingdom[224]

Exercising my position in Christ, I break all agreements with laws, codes and regulations that were made with the ungodly sons of God in all realms, dimensions, and depths.

I break all agreements, covenants and contracts with rebellion that were embedded in those codes, acts, regulations and laws.

I cancel the agreement my ancestors made that gave the enemy the right to make demands on future generations, especially for the purpose of serving darkness and eliminating the light, life, and love of Jesus Christ.

I cancel the written code with all its regulations that were against me and stood opposed to me. I declare that they were nailed to the cross, and that Christ has triumphed over the enemy to the intent that now the manifold wisdom of God might be made known to the rulers and principalities and powers in the heavenly places. May He might expose them to His amazing grace and power.

Lord Jesus, I ask you to reformat our spiritual, physical and soul DNA and RNA, and do a reinstall of the nature and mind of Christ to restore our original design.

Please disconnect me from any ungodly control over the physical elements in my body, and rightly connect me to the physical laws you have established for me.

I exercise my position in Christ and cancel every agreement with all laws and constitutions that were made so that ungodly spiritual stars could have authority.

I repent for my generational line that entered into ungodly governments by writing or endorsing unrighteous laws. I repent for governments that established laws in an attempt to redefine what life was, is, and will be. Lord, I declare you are the only Creator.

I renounce and repent for:
- All human laws that intended to change times and seasons, giving the enemy permission and access to change times and seasons
- All laws that gave the enemy the right to redefine life
- The Supreme Court of the USA that made laws that redefined life, and for all unjust laws that violated the Laws of Almighty God
- Any of my ancestors that were involved in any superior courts' decisions making agreements with evil in order to change the laws and rules of heaven and earth
- My ancestors who initiated new laws and by line upon line, precept upon precept, added layer upon layer of evil laws and practices. Lord, please destroy that system and remove any portion of my spirit or soul that have been trapped in these layers
- Anyone in my generational line that traded future generations for their own protection, power, knowledge and wealth; and who entered into ungodly dimensions to make agreements with fallen sons of God and/or fallen stars. Lord, please break curses off future generations, and restore their original purpose and design. Please remove the ungodly turban, all the blasphemous writings, the ungodly ephod, all ungodly priestly garments, ungodly prayers, declarations and rituals
- All of my ancestors that refused to draw close to the thunder and lightning of the Living God and refrained from entering the holy fear of the Lord
- All those who forsook the Lord and built their own cisterns, choosing mediators of priests and kings rather than intimacy with the Lord

I declare that I give up the kingdoms of this world for the kingdoms of my Christ. Lord, please extract any parts of my spirit out of any ungodly star systems, constellations, and zodiacs out of outer and/or utter darkness, and pull me out of any black holes.

I declare that I will be seated in heavenly places with Christ and my enemies will become my footstool as I rule and reign with Christ; and He will be my God and my Lord. I will not give up my position of ruling and reigning with Christ to the enemy. I will not give up any kingdom; any dimension; any place in time; or any place in, under or above the earth that the Lord has given to me as my sphere of influence.

Lord, please remove the bronze doors and iron bars over my sphere of influence as I say, "Lift up your heads oh you gates that the King of Glory will come in." Please make the crooked places straight, open every door that should be opened, and close every door that should be closed so that the gates will never be shut again.

Lord, please rightly connect my God-given sphere of influence over the multidimensional worlds to other spheres of influence, and allow your power to flow in unity through those spheres.

I declare the kingdoms of this world have become the kingdoms of our Lord and of His Christ, and He shall reign forever and ever! I give You thanks, O Lord God Almighty, the One Who is, Who was, and Who is to come, because You have taken Your great power and reigned.

I declare that salvation and strength, the kingdom of our God, and the power of His Christ have come; for the accuser of our brethren, who accused us before our God day and night, has been cast down. I declare that we have overcome him by the blood of the Lamb and by the word of our testimony, and that we do not love our lives to the death.

I take my position in Christ, and I declare before all the universes, realms and all spiritual beings that I reject the ungodly codes and regulations containing ungodly precepts, laws, rules, writings, decisions, agreements, contracts, covenants that have been written on my DNA and RNA, and I agree with the decision in the throne room of heaven that they be expelled from my body.

I now reject any past claims that my generational line made to these codes and regulations, and I appropriate the blood of Jesus Christ over those codes and regulations as I exchange them for my life in Christ. I choose my rightful inheritance for my life in Christ and my position as a son and heir of my Heavenly Father.

As I am seated with Christ in heavenly places, I choose to live my life according to the blueprints of love that He has written for me before the foundation of the earth.

Father, I declare that I come into alignment with Your Kairos time, and I reject the time of Saturn and Kronos. Lord, if I have been compressed back in time or put into the wrong time line, I agree and declare that I will be in the right time line and ask to be released from any imprisonment so that I am established in the correct time. I demand that I be released, as I am under the Lordship of Jesus Christ, and not under any other gods or goddesses.

I declare that I am not bound by the speed of light but am only bound by the laws of the Kingdom of God.

I declare and agree that I am released to operate in unity with those heavenly laws that are under the Lordship of Jesus Christ and those Kingdoms now belong to Him.

O Lord, the great and awesome God, who keeps his covenant of love with all who love Him and obey his commands, we have sinned and done wrong. We have been wicked and have rebelled. We have turned away from your commands and laws. We have not listened to your servants, the prophets, who spoke in your name to our kings, princes and fathers. Yet, the Lord our God is merciful and forgiving, even though we have rebelled against Him, and have not obeyed Him or kept the laws He gave us through his servants the prophets. Lord, please break the effects of the curses, iniquities, and sworn judgments written in the law of Moses that have been poured out on us and our generational line because we have sinned against you.

Lord, please change all evil addresses that have been installed in the seven eyes of the Lord and please restore them to the original locations that the Almighty God chooses.

APPENDIX

Words from the Lord

It was September 17, 2014 and I had just gone to bed. I thought this book was completed, but I felt a strong urging in my spirit to look at the words the Lord had given us about the sons of God. The next morning I reviewed all those words and was amazed how the Lord had revealed so many truths long before we had even begun to understand the nature of the revealed sons of God.

In our meetings, I would discern the presence of a messenger angel and ask those present receive the message. We documented and saved each message to the computer, a practice that has provided a wonderful historical reference to the unfolding revelation from the Lord. I sense that He desires to instill in us a way of understanding how He speaks, and how he utilizes many in the body of Christ as the recipients of His wisdom. As we treasure and record what He says to us, we are blessed to see how this progressive revelation leads us to a deeper understanding of His majesty and wisdom.

It is essential that I articulate that I do not assume the following words are equal with Scripture. The Word of God is the standard by which we judge every word of revelation we receive. Having said that, I do value what the Lord has spoken and His direction through these words has resulted in a deeper understanding of Scripture.

The words are listed in chronological order, and the identity of each contributor is footnoted. I am so grateful to the Lord for allowing me to have so many friends who love Him. I trust that these words will also help you to understand more of what it means to be a revealed son of God.

March 3, 2008 Jana Green[225]

Some of you were given keys. The table was prepared. Some of you were given to eat at the King's table; preparation for position; the hungry will be satisfied; the thirsty will drink; come and eat, come and drink. Greater purity; buy gold refined in fire. Deeper, deeper still, the deeper things for positioning.
Expand your tent pegs. Gideon's army being prepared. Healing rooms. It is in the depths; deeper still; the deep place where you see His face. Agreement with God and man in the deep place. It is the sons who create co-creators with God in the deep place. There are treasures not yet revealed and saved up for a

time like this. The sons of God revealed. The origin in the deep place. Each of you freely receive, freely give; I am multiplying what you are receiving. Ask for the baptism of fire; greater purity. You have not because you have asked not. This is the transition for the reformation. It is an apostolic order and you are all a part, yet connected. It is a place of supernatural power. You need to operate in it. Get used to it. Get free. So I can release the deep things. Some were given keys, authority in your region, authority in your ministry.

June 2, 2008 Jana Green

It is the ancient pathway; it is the pathway of the righteous that grows brighter and brighter to the full light of day. It is the narrow way; the ancient way to the origin. It is at the origin that the sons of God are revealed. Walk the line. Prepare the way for the sons of God to be revealed. The sons will lead to the Father for His name's sake. Justice for the gate of judgment. Let the son come through, past the Shepherd's rod. It is in the origin that you were knit together. The hope of glory is at hand. It is the path of righteousness for His names sake; it is like going through a birth canal; it is a birthing of something new.

November 18, 2009 Jana Green

You have made it. The next level of transition is here. It is a position of declaration. It is a platform of justice. Don't you know you have been positioned for such a time as this? It has been a time of changing hearts and healing souls. There is unity among you so then you can go. You are under new management.
It has been a time of light affliction, producing a greater glory for the manifestation of the sons of God to be revealed. It is a network connection. The Kingdom has not been what you think. Even the structure has stopped the Kingdom. You are very close; you are on the brink. It is a Kingdom mindset. It is also the heart. Multi-tasking has never been like this before. It is manifold wisdom. Releasing the glory. All connected in the same story. You have learned to know abundance, and you have learned to know a little. You have been faithful in both, and that has been the testing. To be fulfilled in both. You shall not want. There will be no lack.

March 6, 2010 Larry Pearson[226]

Adam had dominion and there is a restoration of Glory. He has given you the authority to release the key for sons and daughters to know their dominion over the prince of the air; for the sons and daughters are called to police the heavens under delegated authority. There is a brand new order being birthed today in the Spirit. There will be a new fire and a new light.

March 21, 2010 Jana Green

This is great grace. If you knew the Kingdom you carry, you would do well. Grace is more than you first believed. It is power to excel, power to believe. You overcome by your testimony, but with grace you are not hindered when you overcome. You are co-creators and co-workers. You have great wealth. It is your time to shine and heal. The revelation of the sons of God. When you stand in opposition, I will give you the words to speak. You will not defend yourself, for heaven is with you and you will be released. Greater is He who is with you than he who is against you. God is with you, carry His name. You will not be stopped or put to shame.

May 25, 2010 Jana Green

You have a perception that in this place where you are reigning, you are over-seeing creation. This is why the godly elohim knew the true co-creators are both sons of God and sons of man. It is for the millennial reign. The true revelation of the true sons, the revealed ones, is for the restoration of creation. The parallel realm was created out of void, of lack. The deception keeps you from achieving the true revelation of who you are. Even in Zechariah, the sons of God did not act. He set the priesthood for Joshua for the new garment. But Zachariah in agreement for heaven proclaimed the new turban for true thinking. It is your thinking that creates. Your co-existence emanates a sound, a color, fragrance, and light. These four are the essence of God. The attempt of the ungodly elohim is to co-create a false perception of God. The false order is in control; it needs to control; it is a perception of order. There is a need for order, and it is a perception of order to control.

So it was in the days of Noah, so it will be in the coming of the son of Man. Even the Nephilim will be in the earth. This war is fought at a cosmic level. Even now, a lie is being dispersed. The counterfeit is at work in the depravity of man. Even the elect will be worn out for the fight to be right. This is why it is said no eye has seen, because it is discerned by the Spirit. The Spirit testifies.

July 5, 2010 Jana Green

A three-strand cord will help you. It is a timeline of deliverance; what was, is, and will be, all tied together to set the captive free. A place of captivity is established by desire. What you hook your eye into will multiply; your sight connected by sound, by fragrance, by light; and around and around. By the foundation of four, seven are revealed. The knowledge of God; a pathway to be recreated to sever the connections. Ungodly connections are still open. The memory is triggered and they come and go, connected by ungodly light. These travel on ungodly light. A jet stream of sound. From the place of captivity, they receive their orders. They hunt and minister by sound and cause disorder. That keeps this one connected and affects the realm.

This is the place of willful trading. What you perceive to believe is traded for what is true in light. You are trading for an inheritance. Where the paths meet. The fallen sons of God are here. The committee behind Satan's argument.

The sons of God to be revealed. You can take your position now. An inheritance fulfilled; what was stolen; what was given away. Ask for the fiery stones to be laid. The Lord is ready to add the fire to the stones, the fire to the incense, the prayers. So the bowls will be poured out. It is not just redemption. It is the vindication of the saints. That is why the enemy is fighting so hard. He must pay back seven fold.

July 13, 2010 Lewis Crompton[227]

Cut off, cut off with the sword. Shatter the tent pegs. Cut off, Cut off. I called them but they wouldn't come. I called My people and they wouldn't come. They brought their gifts, but they wouldn't bring them to me. The gifts were not acceptable to me. I desired a pure heart, but their hearts were not pure. They were not sincere. They didn't understand what I desired. I desired a pure heart. I desired love, and I desired to remove the bonds of oppression from My people; to lift off the bonds of oppression. That is My desire to take off the bonds of oppression from My people, but they could not see that. They could not understand that but they were satisfied to be at the bot-tom of the mountain when I called them up. I said, "Come up higher come up higher." But because of fear and doubt they stayed below. They would not come up to the mountaintop. They were content to worship me by slaughtering goats and lambs, but they would not enter into My presence.

And they worshipped idols of gold and idols of silver, and those broke My heart. And I opened up the heavens over you. And I opened up the heavens to stay over you to think higher and to think bigger, to put aside your rituals. To put aside your sacrifices that I don't accept, and I ask you to come up higher with a pure heart and an open mind, and an open heart to receive My love. Let me enter your heart for I am calling you enter into My heart. I'm calling you to become one with me on this day. On this day, it's all in the heart.

VOLUME 2

We are to lie prostrate before Him and to get rid of our agendas; to be open to new mindsets.

For those who call upon my name, I will make a shift. I will make a shift. I will make a shift in your families. I will make a shift in your organizations. There will be true consecutiveness. Joined. The way I called you to be joined. It will be true connectedness. One mind. One heart. One soul. Unity of the Spirit. Not unity of man, but unity of the Spirit.

They're coming before Him with these packages and they are content to stay at the bottom of the mountain. He's calling them to go higher, but to go higher they have to lay their packages at the feet of the mountain because they aren't the sacrifices God is asking for. It's all in the heart. It's all in the mind. It's in the vision.

He's releasing the Ark of His presence. Now we all have it. It's new structure. New alignment. These are the living stones. This is part of the New Jerusalem; all part of the royal/holy Priesthood. It's part of the New Jerusalem. The structure we are to step out into. Step into His presence while holding the Ark.

I am establishing my people, a royal priesthood. To the ends of the earth they will go, and none will stand against them because none can stand against them. Greater authority than ever before; greater knowledge than ever before; greater wisdom than ever before; greater ability to counsel with me than ever before. For a good friend gives good counsel. And I am a good friend, for my powers are to prosper not to harm. I am establishing good plans. Straight pathways. Acceleration. And I establish in a day this establishment.

I bring structure where there has been disorder and I connect the strength, not the weakness. Break the connections, which have brought you weakness because they are attachments. They are not the whole. For again I will sift your contacts, as you are pure so should your contacts be as they come into alignment with my plans. Not that they would start righteous, but that they would choose righteousness. For my robe fills the temple. It speaks of my majesty.
So I am stretching you out amongst the people group that they would know my majesty and many turn their eyes so they will not see for they have allowed themselves to be blinded by the enemy.

For who is it that sent you? Who was it that gifted you? Who is it that pulled you out? Is it not I? And yet you still do not have faith and yet you still do not trust. Have I not been faithful? From generation to generation and I am faster than you. Sure and steadfast. For you will be an anchor and the presence in the tabernacle of the Lord. For each of you is becoming a warhorse, a horse of breakthrough. I'm establishing My warrior bride and My bride will rise from the ashes with beauty. For you are bringing beauty back to My bride that she will be spotless on the day of My return, for I did not want a sermon but a pure heart. Come under My robe. This is the invitation. And now I speak unto the body, "WAKE UP, WAKE UP!"

For your bridegroom is approaching with justice in His eyes. For He is has been faithful unto the end. Have you been? Return to faithfulness and have no other gods but me. None. Hunger after none but me, for I alone satisfy, and I long to satisfy you. I will remove dissatisfaction from you as you hunger after me. For those who hunger, I will feed. For those who thirst, drink will be given. Strength for the weak. Raise your flags. Raise your flags. Lift up the battle cry and declare the battle is Mine. Declare the victory. Because you have read the book and you know the end. Break off the lies upon My body that they are defeated or that they must wait. For this is a lie. I am bringing acceleration. Is this not the day of the Lord's favor? Why then, would it stop? As you sing, "Worthy unto the lamb," so the lamb sings back. Worthy is the bride. Worthy is the bride. Worthy is the bride.

For blessed are those who overcome Jezebel, for they will not be deceived. Pray for rain in the day of rain. Pray for rain in the day of rain. You will have all things. Do not think I haven't provided; for I already have provided. For though you do not see it, you have all you need. Choose to see differently. Change of perspective. Become righteously retrospective. For who is in you if not the Christ? Who sustains you if not the Christ? For blessing and honor and glory and power belong unto the bride. For that is what I have bestowed upon her. You have not looked to the horizon to see the rising sun. Instead you looked upon your feet at where you were. Lift up you heads. Too long you have not looked unto the hills when your help comes from the Lord, for that was true in David's day, but I came from the hilltops.

Now I choose My earthly vessels. I choose to dwell in the house of men that they would serve Me wholeheartedly. For as they have welcomed me in, so I long to be let out. For Emmanuel is no longer God with us, but God in us. Stop raising your swords to your enemy, for what good is a sword in the hands of a child? Instead turn your hearts and eyes upon me, for the battle is the Lord's; for I arise, I arise and make shouts of joy. For it is the praise of children that silences the foe and the avenger. For your warfare is not a warfare of man or of an earthly realm, but it is of the spirit. For the swords of man have started to fail. For the man-made swords of My people have failed. For they did not use the sword of the Spirit although they thought they were, because they did not speak truth. But they thought they did. Watch your words. Guard your tongue. From out of the overflow of the heart, so a man speaks. Guard your hearts. Treasure me in your hearts. For where your heart is there your treasure is also.

Who have you been spiritually kissing? Who have you been paying lip service to? For lip service is not a service of kings. Though actions may speak louder than words, words create actions and reactions. The population of the remnant is increasing. I will draw them together from near and far, east and west, north and south. That they would raise up a proclamation; though some may doubt and some may hate. This is My person; this is their fate. I am establishing the royal priesthood to take the land and the skies. Their hearts and lives; no compromise; they know their King. They know their God. I'll clothe them with my Ephod.

If you take out the foundation, the building cannot stand. It is you that I am building, My people, My building blocks. For the enemy seeks to destroy from the bottom up, the basic foundations, the elemental basics. They have gone deep beyond molecules. They have made attachments to drain away that which I have given. It takes place even before sin. He seeks to weave himself in the foundation. He has sown himself into the fabric of creation. This is why there is a time to tear. I tore the curtain in the tabernacle between the holy of holies, and so I will tear again My people from the fabric of creation, and the enemy from My new creation. For My people are a new creation; they are not simply those who have confessed My name, but those who truly seek after me. I am separating the wheat from the chaff. Are you ready, are you ready? For I will spit out of My mouth that which is neither hot nor cold. For my hands have been forced, so I will act. For I have previously allowed and covered over with love. I will no longer allow. For the importance and significant for what I will do with a rhythm, as in the days of Ananias and Sapphira.

Cry out like David did so that I will search out your heart, that I will find any offensive way so that you will be free. For My Son makes you righteous, and I see you as righteous. You choose to sin and place yourself in bondage. For you know the consequences. Pick a camp. Pick a camp. Pick a camp and serve wholeheartedly.

The hearts on both sides are strengthening in resolve. Level up. Level up. Go up; go up. Take that all is for you. A face-to-face encounter is coming. Battle face-to-face is coming. You will be opposed in this day to come by the agents of the enemy. You need to know that you will be victorious. It is my will that none will perish. You need to know, you need now. And they will strike first but you will strike last. He sees both sides running down to the valley. The valley belongs to me. You have heard it said, "Fight fire with fire." I say fight with living water. Greater is He who is in you than he who is in the world.

I am releasing the supernatural. Signs and wonders beyond your imagination. Change how you think. Change how you perceive. Fix your foundation. By changing your foundation you create for yourself an ability to maintain all that is impossible through Christ who strengthens you. He is above all things; he is above all things for the benefit of those who seek to serve Him. As you sit next to Him, will his enemies also be your footstools? This is about position and exposition. That which the enemy has brought against you, I will put asunder. I am releasing to you the ability to be the manifested sons of God, the manifested things of God to declare that which is not so that which is; to open the realms; to restore to the Body what has been lost by the occult. I am the redeemer of all things, and that which the enemy has corrupted I will redeem to the fullness and glory of God.

July 15, 2010 Jana Green

Your senses will be accelerated that creation itself may come into agreement with the revealed ones, the true sons. Not just the shift, but a change, a change of mind, change of heart, heaven on earth, is bound to such as these in agree-ment, and you will go down and you will go up, spread wide on the expanse, and trade back for the glory of the sons of man. It is an alignment of engage-ment, trained up and the righteous made perfect, the knowledge of heaven, the knowledge of the realm of glory, the mystery of the Kingdom unfolding, and unfolding, it's now being poured out, and a generation is not yet born, will step into what you are opening, without the waylays, without the destruction, without the warfare, the creative witness, there's a gathering right now of many that have come alongside, of glory assignments, of scrolls being written being changed, being realigned. The DNA is connected to the word on the scrolls, like light, like color, like frequency. Restoring, restoring the souls, even before the womb, you are in communication of an eternal seed. You have authority to declare what not yet has been born, to come in the earth realm and the fullness of their inheritance. You will open, open, open the gates, they're pivotal. At the right time, in the fullness thereof, you will step upon the land when the word comes from above and sound from earth and sound from heaven, sound of earth and sound of heaven. For those who stood firm, for those who held true, the hearts that would change, and the minds that agree. Oh this is wisdom, wisdom from above, wisdom from below, the glory from the center is about to explode, for where you were wrought together, where the substance was made, restoring the DNA to its glory even in this day, for every dot and tiddle is connected to light, to sound, to color, vibration, released above, below and it will be renown, hope in the Almighty, hope also in his works, remembering what you came through, for this is a rebirth.

July 25, 2010 Larry Pearson

The platelets are shifting toward righteousness. For no doubt, the King of Righteousness is being revealed. As the King of righteousness is revealed, I will raise up My sons and daughters with righteousness. They are of a new breed; they are of a new seed. As you stand behind this new breed, they will open up a new path, carve out a new path. They will be like the vanguard to pierce like an arrow into that which has exalted itself against the king of righteousness. They will spread out to the east, west, and north, south. They will become My new compass. This will be multi-dimensional and multi-purposed.

I'm seeing a hurricane-sized whirlwind. What is that Lord? These sons and daughters of righteousness will release a revolution to turn things around; a revolution to bring things full circle; a revolution to open up the timing of the Father; the intention of the Father. Being brought to a new place again, new place again in the spirit; you're going deeper to the right. He's going to show you something of the ancient way, something of the old way. There's a new level of mystery that you're coming into with this room with the ancient blueprints, and I feel it's connected to the unfolding of the Melchizedek order.

August 6, 2010 Larry Pearson

Beauty of Holiness. Beauty of My holiness. In the beauty of My Holiness.
In the womb of the morning. The dawning of the day. The day of the final priesthood. The final priesthood. The final order.

Welcome to My days of the Holy Council where heaven and earth are caught up in the council of the Trinity. Behold, the hour has come where understanding is arriving on the scene that I speak to your spirit and not to your mind. I speak to the Hebrew image and likeness within, and not to the Greek puffed-up mind. Behold, the day of crossing over has come, from the mind and the religious order of man. You have not come to a Christian religion but to One who is love, compassion, and slow to anger. Behold, the day of understanding has come where My father has issued a judgment against the system for that which has been a substitution of the anointed one. This is the hour and era where He is handing over the rule and reign, the true substance of the governing and government council of Kings and Priests. This is the hour that I will catch you up for My foundation has been laid and now, the rest of the story.

Behold, the apostolic has come on the grass-roots revival and reformation of the army of discerners. You will do your part, army of the Most High, as My weapon and My instrument to enlighten My word to the world that I gave over to the sons of men with the light, the new light, and a brighter light than the last reformation. There is now the revelation to see My Son as He really is. Awake oh sleeper, awake and come out from her. Babylon will fall as My Kingdom will swallow every other Kingdom. For you are My kingdom and mountain. You are crossing over from the religious order to the order of Melchizedek. Through identity I will give you new orders and you will be of the ancient order of My warrior where few have gone before. I say now is the time for a company of warriors to arise, a holy nation, a royal priesthood and you will cross a bridge this weekend and you will come into a true identify as who you are as a nation, My nation under God. Lift up your eyes for I will unplug you from the Greek order. I am beginning to unplug your mind from a Greek, man-made mindset. I will birth you into My Hebraic mindset and life. You will know as I know and see as I see. All of these seeds will bear fruit. No word that comes from My mouth will become void but will bear fruit. This is the hour, the convergence. Let go of your conference mentality and addiction, and let go of your other loves. Let go of the lesser thing. For the higher order has come, your High Priest, Your King, Your Lover, Your Bridegroom. You have persevered long. You have pressed beyond the veil. Now rest. See that all that I have is yours. Elder brothers will not tread on this Holy Highway. For this is preserved for true sons and daughters that are robed in true sonship. This is the hour. Keep chronicling the light for it will accelerate. Listen with your spirit. Take heed with the anointing I have given you within, for it is true. Learn to listen with your heart more, and you will soar on the wings of the Word and the Word will discern the thoughts and intentions and motivations and it will divide asunder the hirelings and sons of the Kingdom.

November 13, 2010 Larry Pearson

My eye of counsel; a convergence of counsel; entering into the counseling chamber, listen with your heart; listen with your heart. Through many dangers, many toils, I have brought you through, I have brought you through. Heavens are excited, the heavens are excited, prepare your heart for an upgrade. Your weapons of old will not work in the new. I have already released from heaven an armory, a new upgrade of armory is at hand. I am setting My people in place, My army in place. This will be a brand new race. May you find the rest of the story; may you find me, your Rest, in the story. Coming through, it might seem dark but there's radiance on the other side. In the spirit and in the natural, all things are made new. I've had to bring you through to a broader and spacious, bigger place. Be not afraid to move your tent, be not afraid to pull up your tent pegs. For I am with you, be afraid of nothing. I am calling for the dread champions, fearless ones, filled with My heart and courage. The spirit of Elijah will carry you through and bring you to the sons and daughters that I've called you to. The veil is being lifted; the veil is being lifted; the veil of what was is being lifted. Look not to yesterday, because yesterday is dead and gone.

February 11, 2011 Larry Pearson

Magnetic north is not true north. This day I bring a shift to displace and re-place the foundations of idol worship, satanic worship. This day I have writ-ten a decree. This day I loose a scroll on all four points of this region. I am replacing the exaltation of the Mayan spirit, of the Mayan altars, of the ancient ungodly ways. I will send My breath, My Holy breath through My holy people to topple towers. The day of exposure has come. The day of My deliverer has arrived. This day the unrighteous compass shall be shattered, and I now issue a decree of a righteous compass and shall establish true north. A company of freedom fighters shall come forth. A kingdom quaking for a holy awakened people. A generation of Jonah being expelled from the belly of religion. A day of true liberty. A day of true freedom. A day of alignment. A day of assignment. Established from heaven to earth. Do not fear evil but trust in what is good and true. A tearing down of false powers. Establishing sons of the Kingdom. Champions born of the realm. Great wonders and signs will be born out of the sons of the Kingdom. Together we fly, together we soar.

Fresh understanding of what has been bought. Your eyes of understanding shall be filled with new light of what I have accomplished for My day of might.

Evil waters recede. Evil waters recede. Shrink back. Be no more. For now is the time, yes My lions shall roar. Take dominion. Take dominion. Execute dominion. Through lifestyle you see. It shall shatter the myths of the want-to-bees. Through lifestyle you shall see the fullness of Me.

May 29, 2011 Jana Green

In servitude to access the gates, the great exchange. For what was shut will be opened and what was opened will be shut. You will go in and you will go out and change the region. Restore the DNA so the sons of God may be revealed. Your senses will be accelerated. That creation itself will come into agreement with the true ones, the true sons. Not just a shift, but also a change; a change of mind; a change of heart. Heaven on earth is bound to such as these in agreement. You will go down and you will go up. Spread wide on the expanse and trade back for the glory of the sons of man. It is alignment of engagement. Trained up and the righteous made perfect, the knowledge of heaven, the knowledge of the realm of glory, the mysteries of the Kingdom unfolding. It is now being poured out. A generational not yet born will step into what you are opening, without the way-lays, without the destruction, without the war-fare. Creative witness. There is a gathering right now of many who have come alongside. Glorious assignments. Scrolls being written, changed, realigned.

The DNA is connected to the word on the scroll; the frequencies, the colors, vibrations, and the sounds. Restoring the souls even before the womb. You are in communication of the eternal seed. You have the authority to declare of what yet has not been born to come into the earth realm the fullness of their inheritance. You will open, open, open the gates. They are pivotal. At the right time, in the fullness of time, you will step onto the land when the word comes from above. The sound from earth and the sound from heaven will connect the arc of power.

I will set the four-fold foundation, the anchor of the throne for righteousness and justice will be made known. The wheel within the wheel will again sit on the earth. You will go where the spirit goes and you will go in rebirth. My eyes go to and fro for those who are coming through; for those who stood firm; for those who held true, the hearts that where changed, the minds that agreed.

Wisdom from above, and wisdom from below; the glory from the center is about to explode. Where you were wrought together, where the substance was made restoring the DNA to its glory even in this day. Every dot and tittle is connected to light, sound, the color and vibrations. Released from above, and below and it will be renown. Hope in the Almighty. Hope also in His work; remembering what you came through, for this is a rebirth.

June 18, 2011 Jana Green

Keep shifting. Keep moving. It is the holy way. When you step into the gates you open the expanse. It is wider still for a greater advance.

It is a step of faith. It opens up the realms. You must learn and experience the way of the width and expanse. Many will trust, and many maneuver and create from this realm the stewardship of the Creator God; it is given to man. I want to release the anointing of greater works. You trust in me, trust also in the works that I do. So your mind is expanded. Your imagination will ring true. Sanctified to the holy words by the sounds of the creator; shifting, going in and out. The mystery is hard to explain. Stay where you are, but I move you for the Kingdom in the realm. You have been set aside like a holy abandonment. Not that you are orphans, but I have tested the heart to seek my face; to seek the face of the Holy One. To reveal the mystery of the God of Daniel who is his judge. Practice. Learn in this way. Experience. It is a platform of justice that you may agree; change in heaven and earth that you may agree. Build on what you learn for the acceleration of wisdom. I am pouring out My spirit on all flesh. The divine remnant is to know the mystery through heaven and earth, the supernatural creative mystery of the true witness of Yahweh. For the true sons are in the earth, the revealed ones.

October 25, 2011 Larry Pearson

Answering the call of wisdom breaks open the box where the treasures have been hidden. Many newer keys. Learn from a bended knee how to see Me, wisdom. Teach them to heed me, wisdom. I am unlocking ancient mysteries at this time to unhook the sons of man, to redeem creation. As the sons of men awake to the true identity of the sons of God, creation will quake as it awakes. Behold, I do all things well. I take what is an entrapment and make it like a womb to birth the treasures out of darkness. Identity reborn.

October 15, 2011 Larry Pearson

A restoration of sons; a restoration of true manhood; a reversing of ancient curses; a restoration of a true warrior spirit, a warrior spirit of love, a warrior spirit of compassion, a warrior spirit of true tender mercies and a displacement of an anti-Christ spirit. Who are these uncircumcised Philistines anyway? There are giant slayers in the room. You will slay them by the breath of your love. You will slay them by your deeds of kindness. The foundations are quaking and there is a re-making of true men of love, compassion, tender hearted in the nature and presence of Christ within. Look up, your redeemer has drawn nigh. I am the Lord of the sea and I will make the nations see that I am the Lord of the sea.

October 13, 2011 Larry Pearson

It's a watershed moment; preparation of a people to ride into new heights and new dimensions to open up a hidden gate. The mountain of the Lord is to be unveiled; a preparation of a people to dwell among the mountain of rest to know my best, to hear and to know, to know and to hear. This is a strategic time on the Father's clock. The sons of my kingdom will build the brightness of the glorious ones rising and shining as a beacon of great light. There is a golden oil to be poured out upon the people; much freedom, much freedom.

There's a convergence, a convergence of anointing, of offices for the hour of restoration of a people for reformation to be brought out of the old, to behold the new. Strategic time to come and dine; the hidden things are now going to be revealed.

Horses: there's a dispatch of swift horses, swift horses, into the realms of acceleration. Discernment, discernment, discernment; with the keys of discernment you will unlock sickness and disease off the people. There are healing wells in the land, healing wells in the land. People are being prepared as healers of a new breed.

October 25, 2011 Larry Pearson

Baby blue. Robin egg blue. There are eggs for you. Eggs in a nest. Here comes My best. As you sit and wait I will hatch the great. Come to the heights. There are legal rights to birth the new. There are documents for you. Training for reigning through the ancient way at the feet of the Ancient of Days. Enter My rest and hatch the best. As you believe, you will receive marching orders. They are waiting in the wings. A new dispatch of beings. An army of saints rising to new heights of stature. Sons of the Kingdom. Mature by nature and by reason of use. This is the time to be back to the future. Back to go forward. Mothers and fathers. Sons and daughters. Title deeds for the family, the sons and daughters. Out of your loins come world changers, culture breakers. I'm releasing a new vibration to touch a nation, a holy nation

October 25, 2011 Jana Green

It is a culmination, a merging of two. The realm of heaven and of earth, culminating. They taught this army arising by the righteous made perfect. Heaven has been waiting a long time for this day, for the sons of God to take their position in the authority of the armies of the Lord. It is for the land's sake, for Israel's sake, for heaven's sake. There are those being raised up in the earth, those who are called Holy. Some are being trained in secret. Some are being given more strategy. Downloads of divine intervention so the kingdoms of this world will become the kingdoms of our Lord. It is a culmination.

May 22, 2012 Jana Green

It has been given you to know the right of passage, the safe way, the highway; to know the authority of the Kingdom of God. Let the redeemed say so, for the Kingdom of Heaven is at hand. And it was for Elisha to pray for rain. It was first noticed, a cloud the size of a man's hand. All authority for the King-dom of God is at the hand of man. So the eye of the Lord is on Israel, the city of the great King, Jerusalem. The Prince of Peace is always the head of the government, and there will be no end. You are called to Mt. Zion, to the

New Jerusalem, to the myriad of angels. This is the order, the protocol; to the general assembly; to God, the judge; to the spirit of righteous men, made perfect; to Christ, the mediator and the sound of the Blood which speaks a better word. For the council of God is in the revealed sons. This order, this government, is aligned to the spirit of righteous men made perfect. For what was, is and will be now. You are the connector that releases the creative realm of heaven on earth. So what is bound on heaven is bound on earth? The true order of government. Open, open, open, open. Gates, like in a corridor. Opening, opening, opening. There is a government of rule established by gates. Some are the mind of man. Others were heaven's gates. A sphere of influence. A ruling yet determined to turn back the battle. You are coming through them.

June 30, 2012 Jana Green

The watchers are aligned with authority that go in and out for the communica-tion between the saints and the earth to inform heaven. They are all about. Creation is subject to the creature, the true authority in the earth. Your author-ity stands in your identity and your worth. The sons of God are the ones who obtain the resurrection from the dead; for all family in heaven and in earth derived their name, grow up into the head. Color is an entity where frequen-cies go in and out. Vibration is what it is all about. Many frequencies make up a color; they go in and out. They change as a chromatic prism. The sons of God are the ones who reveal the image, for the Kingdom of God dwells within. You are the divine image to release heaven for that is where it begins. The color is tied to the frequencies, the divine partaker of the divine image. For everything in life and government have been given to the sons. For healing has been given, now begun. There is a time coming, and is now here, for the sons of God to be revealed. Much has been said, and more to come, for the divine nature to be revealed. The creation is subject to futility to him who subjected it, in hope that the manifest present would be recreated. The true authority in earth has been given to the sons of men. To know who you are is the divine plan. So as a man thinks, by desire within how he perceives positions him. The greater authority is within. Learn more from the certain one, the frequencies of heaven, and the frequencies of the son.

August 7, 2012 Lewis Crompton

Open hearts, open minds. Time to undo the devil's crime. I have been waiting an age and a half to kill the bull, to kill the calf. Are you ready for the great ex-pose? I give it on a platter; I give it on a tray. It is the glory of God to conceal a matter. And with revelation comes the power to shatter. Only to my sons I reveal what is hidden. I tell you no lies, I am not kidding. This is revelation for the time and for the season. I am manifesting beyond your reason. The enemy has been committing high treason. The dead has been dead; dead too long. I am releasing the secrets to life; the building blocks to resurrection; the precepts to manifestation; that you might walk like Jesus, sons in perfect relationship. Perception is not an ideal it is a reality. Perfection is a location and an accreditation. Perception is a location. Shift your location. Shift your perception. Raise a hallelujah.

Flags still fly at night but can only be seen in a day. The sun is rising to expose the pirate's flag; too many pirates in the fellowship. Uncross your bones and put down your stones. There is a better way to communicate than with stones. I am calling the remnant; it is a different frequency, a different sound. It is coming up through the earth, it is giving birth. Watch, for the land is starting to groan. The plants are now growing that I have sown. These are the gears of war; the cogs of decision; prayers bring precision. The enemy has laid siege but My people will be free. Are you brave enough to declare war with the Captain of the Host?

[The fallen sons of God] are thieves. They are robbers of the riches. They are stealers of sovereignty. They are masquerades. They are deceivers. They have representatives on the earth [in] positions of high authority. They are in your government. They are embodied in bodies on the earth. They have human counterparts, human hosts. They have children, and they have wives. They are mockers of God. They have grafted themselves into your DNA. Sick-ness comes from them. Defeat them, defeat sickness. They are the designers of cancer and the makers of mental illness. They bring sorrow and suffering. You overcome them by overcoming suffering. This is why Christ's authority was made perfect by suffering. Perfection is disconnection from the fallen

108

sons. Perfection is connection with the perfect Son. If your eye causes you to sin, remove it from the camp of the enemy. Gouge it out from the grip of the fallen. God wants to undo the agreement made with the fallen sons of God, a covenant made with the enemy that is more ancient than God's covenant. They do not know whom they are dealing with. Think of the havoc that one fallen son brought, and times it by a billion. I am releasing a deeper revelation of sonship to those who inherit the Kingdom. True sons spot false sons. A true son doesn't just take, but works in his father's estate.

I am receiving instruction from the Father. Listen to My instructions, My son. Time to come up and out of this place. Time to be released from the enemy's camp. You have been prisoners of war.

Some people say there is no war. I will ask them, "How do you think a Kingdom is established?" For I will rule and reign over every place, kingdom, realm and dimension.

I see a basket with blueprints. Larry Pearson continues:

The kingdom is here. I've opened up a gate. I'm raising My hand. You are part of My hand, to touch the land, to become My fingers, to execute kingdom reality into the land by My hand. An anointing to see. The appointing of the fingers of God, the fingers of God to bring judgment against the systems.

The ancient systems shall fall. This is the hour where your heart will be full of power to see as I see, to be what I've called you to be. Your heart will bow and break for this is the hour for a spiritual quake. This is the time for the body of Christ to chime in time. This is the race, this is a new race, this is a new race, and this is not a sprint. This is not a sprint. This is a relay, a generational relay race for the counsel is here to give a baton to whoever has been chosen. Let the runners rise up in the desert; let the runners rise up in the desert. All hands on deck. End time runners, generational runners, generational occupation. The true occupiers will run with the baton of the Ancient of Days and run and find the ancient ways. The Chief of all chiefs has come to redeem the land, to reveal His hand. He's not here to takes sides. He's here to take over, for no longer will there be a company that's divided. They will rise with a staff and they will be a generation of power, of glory, of love, love, love... runners of love, Father's love, quaking and baking. The saint, you are in the oven of your Father. You think its hot now, get ready; there's a heat wave that has touched this continent. The glory of the Father has rested upon a continent that will bake and shake with the Father's love, for Elijah has unlocked the oven of God. He will refine you and define you, oh continent, on North America you will bake, you will quake in the fire of Perfect Love that will drive out all fear. The orphanage will fall into the sea and the sons of God and the counsel of God and the commissioning of God and the lively stones will be built upon one another. Days of habitation are coming. He's calling for the collective to come, the collective of the household of the Father built by the Spirit, and it will displace the system, the orphan system, and it will be the family of God.

August 7, 2012 Dawn Bray[228]

Today I have brought you into the land of the living. I have redeemed another place in the depth. I call you to walk as sons of God attached to the perfect Son of God, radiating His glory. Healing will manifest from this revelation. Relationships will be restored. This is a building block. Precept upon precept, line upon line, I will reveal the pieces. I will release connectors and make di-vine connections. I am restoring My divine order, My government, My Kingdom, My ways. It has been a very good day.

August 18, 2012 Jana Green

Declare to the realms; take up your position; declare to the realms. All must bow to the resurrected ones, these are the true sons, the revealed ones. It is easier than you think. The mighty must bow to the true sons, the revealed ones. Just take a drink. For the kingdom of heaven is at hand. Declare to creation; declare to the land. What you choose here, a judgment will proclaim. From heaven to earth, I will release My name. Restoration is mine. The ad-ministration is mine. The regeneration is mine. The generations are mine. Let the stones cry out, for heaven is heard. There is agreement in the land. The resurrection plan. Your perception is changing for what you see you will believe. The Lord is good. Oh, He is Good.

August 25, 2012 Jana Green

A council awaits with a platform of justice. Not a city council, not a government council, but a heavenly one for judgments. A certain one with two others is here among you to come over. A platform awaits to touch. Move the sons. Justice will be served for the resurrected ones. The true sons. A remnant revealed will be heard. Heaven awaits to engage the true sons. The sound, the sound. The Lion from Zion has now come.

October 11, 2012 Rob Gross

There is a new release of power and authority coming upon My people to speak forth the gospel in a new way. For the darkness is being removed, and My light is beginning to bubble forth. What the enemy meant for wrong I am turning to My people's good. For in ancient days past, I fathered the mighty heroes of the earth, but in this hour, I am fathering and releasing My sons and daughters and they shall be mighty heroes as well. I am sounding a trumpet that will release a sound that will gather people on an international scope to embrace the shift in the atmosphere. A new season; a new day; a new dimension; the expansion of My Kingdom to the ends of the earth.

November 13, 2012 Lewis Crompton

It's a culture of music; it's a culture of praise. Singing about the blood of Him who was raised. Learning to be sons, learning to be heirs. Learning to cast away the world and its cares. I'm bringing you in to a broader place; I'm revealing it to you face to face. It's not for the one; it's for the many. This is the fruit; this is the berry. More wine, more wine, more wine; I'm coming with a sign. It's time to fall into line. It's time to discover the old plumb line. I'm drilling down; I'm drilling deep; the climb is fast the climb is steep. It's a learning curve like never before. You're going to learn to access my store. Open the gate; open the door. There's always more; there's always more. Friends are free, and you're free from friends. I'm straightening out the ungodly bends. It's time to oscillate, time to shift; when searching for gold you have to sift.

First you seek; then you find; you're searching for a particular kind. When you've found, then you weigh. You cannot weigh what you have not found. How do you weigh a sound? You can't. I'm moving you forward down the road; this is the fruit of what you have sowed.

November 14, 2012 Lewis Crompton

Conduits of power
This is a tower of power
This is the hour of power
The time has come for what needs to be done
To reveal the glorious Son
Take of the earmuffs
Open the old bulkheads
Remove the false capstones and light a fire
Stay in the presence
Stay in the dwelling place

It starts and ends in the tabernacle Holy of holies

Holy is holy

Clouds of reckoning Clouds of redeeming

Hundreds are coming but hundreds are screaming

I want My people's cries to be louder than the screams The tears have been made for streams

Streams of healing

This river flows up, flows up stream towards the throne, towards the King, towards the sun

Re-think the prodigal son

For he was re-awoken to his understanding of his sonship That he was a son of the Father, a son of God,

As he was in the beginning So he will be in the end.

Was the son who stayed really a son if he never knew the Father?

So I am bringing you home

Out of the swine pit

Come out from amongst the swine For I have walked you into maturity I have walked you into revelation

And I have brought you to this destination For this revelation

For the sons of God are to be revealed And the enemy is to be kneeled

His ownership is being repealed And his fate has already been sealed Time to win

There is no time for sin No time to lose

Now you can stop losing Stop losing time

The great unwashed will become washed And those that are unclean will become seen As I reveal my true sons

They are not days of darkness they are days of clarity Where dark is seen for dark and light is seen for light Though deception may reign you will know the truth

This has been my purpose, that you would not be deceived

Though the end may be nigh I will keep you up high

November 2, 2012 Jana Green

By the Spirit, by the Spirit, the promise. Born of the freed woman is Isaac, the promised. Sent to redeem flesh by the regeneration, by the washing endowed with the Spirit. You heard you are all sons, and so you are. You are all gods, and so you are. From the place of origin, from where you start. You must agree to want this. You must agree to know. You inheritance is given to you, all written on a scroll. Before one day came to pass, it was yours. But it was traded, so it was altered.

If you have followed Me through this regeneration, you will all sit on thrones and judge the sons of Israel. What you have given up for My sake, you will restore what was lost and all that was lost will come in place. Catching up. It lies dormant. The treasures within the Kingdom of God. The Kingdom of God is within, that is where it begins. You lost sight of the goal before time came to pass. Your inheritance was rich when you perceived lack. By sound and light your frequency, your vibration. It is about the stones. It is about regeneration.

It's been given to you to trade back the DNA. For the order of Melchizedek has made this day. The sound begets light, the creative force. For transference is waiting, transference for the course. Creation itself is groaning and Zion can't wait. For these standing here have been waiting for the revealing of the sons, so it's not too late. Your position was sure; the covenant was made. Renounce the other covenants, for this is the day. It's being written, its being recorded now. These were the crowns; take what is yours. The government at the gate, what's given in marriage, it's not too late.

GLOSSARY

Ahab--*An evil king of Israel; married to Jezebel; opened the spiritual gates of Israel to the demonic influence of Baal at a level not seen before*

Apokalupsis—*Greek word for revealing; disclosure; appearing, coming, enlighten, make naked or uncover, and has to do with the exposing of something that has been hidden from view, or bringing into the light that which has been kept in obscurity*

Amraphel—*King of Shinar; may be Nimrod*

Anakim—*A people regarded as giants; hybrid mixture of man and an elohim*

Angelos—*Greek for angel; messenger*

Apis—*Egyptian god of sacred bull, or cow god (cattle): also known as Hathor*

Apokaradokia—*Greek for expectantly; meaning 'to wait with the head raised and the eye fixed on that point of the horizon from which the expected object is to come'*

Arioch—*King of Ellasar; means servant of the moon god; may have been the grandson of Nimrod*

Ashteroth—*Female sun god; also known as Shamash*

Baal—*Semitic noun meaning lord, owner, or master; the supreme god worshipped in Canaan and Phonecia; considered to be the leader of the Rephaim; a fertility god; also known as Yerah, Apollo, Jupiter, Nimrod and Saturn; involved ritualistic prostitution in the temples and human sacrifice, usually the firstborn of the one making the sacrifice; prince of the underworld*

Babylon—*Gateway of the god; city founded by Nimrod* **Bashan**—*Golan; region where Rephaim lived; means the place of the serpent* **Ben-Ammi**—*Son of Lot; founding father of the Amonites*

Bene [ha] elohim—*Hebrew for sons of God* **Bera**—*King of Sodom; Bera means son of evil*

Birsha—*King of Gomorrah; Birsha means sons of wickedness* **Brephos**—*Greek for infant*

Chedorlaomer—*King of Elam; means servant of Lagamar, a goddess in the Elamite pantheon*

Chemosh—*A god to whom child sacrifice was made*

Chiun—*A god associated with Saturn*

Children of God—*Sons of God who have been redeemed by Jesus' blood* **Ellasar**—*May have been located in southern Babylon*

Elohim—*Hebrew for God (singular)*

elohim (note small e)—*Hebrew for gods (plural); beings that inhabit the spiritual plane of reality*

Emim—*A people regarded as giants by the Moabites*

Eres—*Hebrew word for earth; also rendered in certain contexts as Sheol or the Under-world*

Fallen sons of God—*Those who mated with daughters of men to produce Nephilim*

Fractal—*A rough or fragmented geometrical shape that can be subdivided in parts, each of which is (at least approximately) a smaller copy of the whole; a never ending pattern*

Geb—*Egyptian god of earth (gnats)*

Golgotha—*Means the place of the skull; possible burial ground of Goliath; place of Jesus' crucifixion*

Goliath—*Philistine warrior; a giant; an Anakim; may mean to uncover, remove or go into exile or may indicate the revealing of someone, a secret or message*

Hades—*The Greek underworld (substituted for)* **Hapi**—*Egyptian god of the Nile River (water)*

Haran—*Site of the temple of moon god, Sin; place where Terah eventually settled*

Hathor—*Egyptian god of sacred bull, or cow god (cattle); also known as Apis* **Heqt**—*Egyptian goddess of birth (frogs)*

Huios—*Greek for mature, fully developed sons who have come of age into full maturity*

Huiothesia—*Greek for sonship, referring to the standing or position of a son who has the rights and privileges of inheritance; adoption as sons*

Isangeloi—*Greek phrase, 'for they are equal to the angels'*

Iselle—*Hebrew for devoted to God; Turkish for moonbeam or moon like* **Ishtar**—*The queen of heaven*

Isis—*Egyptian goddess of healing (boils)*

Jericho—*The City of the Moon; spiritual center for star worship in Canaan*

Jeroboam—*First king over Israel after the split from Judah*

Jezebel—*Wife of King Ahhab; daughter of King Ethbaal of the Sidonians; name means "Where is the Prince?", a ritual cry from worship ceremonies honoring Baal; as queen, attempted to kill the prophets of God while raising up 450 prophets of Baal and 400 prophets of Asherah*

Julio—*Spanish for downy-bearded, soft haired, implying youthful* **Katartizo**—*Greek for equip, meaning to mend the nets*

Kheper—*Egyptian god of beetles (flies)*

King of Bela—*King of Zoar; Bela means destruction* **Lupus**—*Latin for wolf*

Melchizedek—*The eternal High Priest, who later came as Jesus Christ; King of Peace (Salem); King of Righteousness*

Misr—*A derivative of Mizraim, Noah's grandson; Egyptians* **Moab**—*Son of Lot; founding father of the Moabites*

Moloch—*Chief deity over the Canaanites; a fallen son of God; king; a god to whom child sacrifice was made*

Mount Carmel—*Site where the prophet Elijah defeated the prophets of Baal and Asherah*

Nachash—*Hebrew adjective for shining one; serpent*

Nephilim—*Offspring of fallen sons of God and daughters of men; giants* **Nimrod**—*Great grandson of Noah; evil*

Nut—*Egyptian goddess of the sky (hail)*

Orphanos—*Greek word for orphan, and is translated comfortless*

Pantheon—*Gods of the nations on earth, or 'gods of the peoples'; fallen sons of God*

Pharoah—*Egyptian chief god of Egypt (firstborn)* **Ra**—*Egyptian sun god (darkness)*

Rehoboam—*Solomon's son who succeeded him as King; so evil that God split the kingdom into Judah and Israel, removing 10 tribes from his authority*

Rephaim--*Hebrew word translated as ghosts of the dead; shades; the sunken ones or those who dwell in the netherworld; giants; departed spirits*

Rephan—*The Assyrian god of Saturn; perhaps refers to the Egyptian Saturn god Repa*

Samsung—*Korean word meaning three stars, with three representing something big, numerous and powerful; and stars meaning eternity*

Saturn—*The star god*

Seth—*Egyptian god of crops (locusts)*

Shamash—*Female sun god of the Canaananites; consort of Yerah; name later changed to Ashteroth*

Shemeber—*King of Zeboiim; Means lofty flight*

Sheol—*Hebrew word for the underworld*

Shinab—*King of Admah; tied to the moon god, meaning sin is my father*

Shinar—*Probably identical to Babylonia or Southern Mesopotamia* **Sikkuth**—*Babylonian reference to Saturn*

Sonship—*A state of position, not salvation; grants us the authority to release the Kingdom of God on earth*

sons of disobedience (note small s)—*Mentioned in Ephesians 2:2*

sons of God (note small s)—*Created spiritual beings that can be fallen or revealed*

Son of God (note capital S)—*Jesus, the Only Begotten Son of God*

Star of the morning—*Identified in KJV as Lucifer*

Teknon—*Adolescents*

Terah—*Father of Abraham; settled in Ur* **Theos**—*Greek for God*

Tidal—*King of nations; possible Hittite connection*

Ungodly length—*A spiritual place within the heavenly realms where the orphan resides*

Ur—*City of the moon*

Valley of Rephaim—*Valley of Giants, or Valley of Departed Spirits* **Yerah**—*Moon god; chief god of the Caananite pantheon; name later changed to Baal* **Yada**—*Hebrew for knew*

Y'rn-sha-lah-yim—**Jerusalem***; Yara, the first half of Jerusalem, means to cast, direct or instruct as in 'the way to go through'; Shalem, the second half of Jerusalem means 'to be made complete, to make amends, restitution or restore'*

Zamzummim—*A people regarded as giants by the Ammonite*

*END NOTES

Chapter 1

1. Also, *Rephan* and *Romphan*

2. Kaiwan – perhaps meaning shrine

3. Oswalt, J. N. (1999). 1491. In R. L. Harris, G. L. Archer, Jr. & B. K. Waltke (Eds.), *Theological Wordbook of the Old Testament* (R. L. Harris, G. L. Archer, Jr. & B. K. Waltke, Ed.) (electronic ed.) (623). Chicago: Moody Press.

4. Gooding, D. W. (1996). Kaiwan. In D. R. W. Wood, I. H. Marshall, A. R. Millard, J. I. Packer & D. J. Wiseman (Eds.), *New Bible dictionary* (D. R. W. Wood, I. H. Marshall, A. R. Millard, J. I. Packer & D. J. Wiseman, Ed.) (3rd ed.) (642). Leicester, England; Downers Grove, IL: InterVarsity Press.

5. Oswalt, J. N., *Theological Wordbook of the Old Testament*, 623

6. Wikipidia, The Free Encyclopedia; http://en.wikipedia.org/wiki/Samsung

7. Moloch, Molekh, Molok, Molek, Molock, or Moloc

8. Also, Milcom, National god of the Ammonites

9. Myers, A. C. (1987). *The Eerdmans Bible Dictionary* (728). Grand Rapids, MI: Eerdmans.

10. Strong, J. (2001). *Enhanced Strong's Lexicon.* Bellingham, WA: Logos Bible Software.

11. 2 Kings 21:1-6, 2 Chronicles 28:1-4

12. Acts 7:43

13. Herrmann, W. (1999). Baal. In K. van der Toorn, B. Becking & P. W. van der Horst (Eds.), *Dictionary of deities and demons in the Bible* (K. van der Toorn, B. Becking & P. W. van der Horst, Ed.) (2nd extensively rev. ed.) (131–139). Leiden; Boston; Köln; Grand Rapids, MI; Cambridge: Brill; Eerdmans.

14. Ibid., 131-139.

15. Ibid., 131-139

16. Hosea 2:16–20

Chapter 2

17. Lupus is the Latin word for wolf.

18. The adverb 'before' is the same as in Genesis 2:5, "...*when there was not yet a shrub of the field...and the Lord God had not yet sent rain upon the earth*". in Jeremiah 1:5, "*before I formed you in the womb...*" is the same verb as in Genesis 2:7.

118

Chapter 3

19. For a discussion about the other possible translations of Nephilim, see Michael Heiser, *The Myth That Is True*, p. 85-94

20. Job 1:6–7

21. Job 2:1–2

22. Job 38:4–7

23. Heiser, Michael. (2006-2012). *The Myth that is True*, p. 96ff.

Chapter 4

24. 2 Peter 2:4-5

25. Jude 5-7

26. There are many writers who refer to the *Book of Enoch* to support the idea of the sons of God being angels. I have chosen not to rely on any extra-Bibli-cal sources.

Chapter 5

27. There are other scriptures that use the word elohim that may indicate the righteous sons of God: **Genesis 23:5–6:** *And the sons of Heth answered Abraham, saying to him, "Hear us, my lord: You are a mighty [elohim] prince among us; bury your dead in the choicest of our burial places. None of us will withhold from you his burial place, that you may bury your dead."*

Exodus 7:1: *So the Lord said to Moses: "See, I have made you as God [elohim] to Pharaoh, and Aaron your brother shall be your prophet. You shall speak all that I command you. And Aaron your brother shall tell Pharaoh to send the children of Israel out of his land."* **Exodus 9:28**: *Entreat the Lord, that there may be no more mighty [elohim] thundering and hail, for it is enough. I will let you go, and you shall stay no longer.*

Exodus 21:5–6: But if the servant plainly says, "I love my master, my wife, and my children; I will not go out free," then his master shall bring him to the judges [elohim]. He shall also bring him to the door, or to the doorpost, and his master shall pierce his ear with an awl; and he shall serve him forever.

Exodus 22:8: *If the thief is not found, then the master of the house shall be brought to the judges [elohim] to see whether he has put his hand into his neighbor's goods.*

1 Samuel 4:7–8: So the Philistines were afraid, for they said, "God has come into the camp!" And they said, "Woe to us! For such a thing has never happened before. Woe to us! Who will deliver us from the hand of these mighty gods [elohim]? These are the gods [elohim] who struck the Egyptians with all the plagues in the wilderness.

Psalm 136:2: *Oh; give thanks to the God of gods [elohim]! For His mercy endures forever.*

28. *Theological dictionary of the New Testament.* 1964- (G. Kittel, G. W. Bromiley & G. Friedrich, Ed.) (electronic ed.). Grand Rapids, MI: Eerdmans.

29. See also Ephesians 2:2, 'sons of disobedience.'

30. Day, C. A. (2009). *Collins Thesaurus of the Bible.* Bellingham, WA: Logos Bible Software.

31. See also: Exodus 21:5-6, 22:8–11, 22:20, 23:13, 32:1; Deuteronomy 4:28–29, 5:6–7, 6:14, 7:4, 8:19, 10:17–18, 13:2, 13:6, 13:13, 17:3, 28:14, 29:26, 30:17, 31:18–21, 32:17; Joshua 24:2, 24:14–16; Judges 2:12–13, 17, 19, 5:8, 6:31, 8:33, 10:13–14, 17:5–6; 1 Samuel 14:15, 26:19, 28:13; 1 Kings 9:5–6, 11:3–4, 14:9, 18:27, 19:2, 20:10; 2 Kings 5:7, 17:7, 17:35–39, 19:18, 22:17; 1 Chronicles 16:25; 2 Chronicles 13:8–9, 25:14, 28:25, 34:24–25; Psalm 8:5, 82:1–7, 95:3, 96:4, 97:7–9; Isaiah 41:23; Jeremiah 1:16, 2:11, 7:6, 7:18–19, 11:10–12, 16:11–13, 19:4, 19:12–13, 22:9, 25:6–7, 32:29, 35:15–16, 44:3–8; Ezekiel 28:1–9; Hosea 3:1; Malachi 2:15

Chapter 6

32. Job 1:6

33. Wikipedia, The Free Encyclopedia; http://en.wikipedia.org/wiki/Conspiracy_theory

34. Genesis 1:26-27

35. Heiser, Michael, *So, What Exactly is an Elohim?* p. 4

36. Hebrews 12:9

37. Ibid, Michael Heiser, p.4

38. Jeremiah 1.5

39. Genesis 3:6-7

40. Genesis 2:7

41. Otis, George Jr., (1997). *The Twilight Labyrinth* (pp. 96-99). Grand Rapids, Michigan: Chosen Books.

42. Genesis 2:15

43. Genesis 2:9, 16-17; 3:1-6, 11-12

44. Genesis 3:9-10

45. Genesis 3:1-5

46. Genesis 3:19-20

47. Genesis 1:26-28

48. Otis, George Jr., *The Twilight Labyrinth*, p. 105

49. Luke 3:23-28

50. Genesis 3:14-15

51. 1 Corinthians 15:45-48

Chapter 7

52. Genesis 6:5-7

53. Creation Tips; http://www.creationtips.com/flooddate.html

54. Genesis 6:8

55. Genesis 6:10

56. Luke 3:23-38

57. Leviticus 18:1-30

58. The ungodly length was introduced in Volume 1 and will be discussed further in succeeding volumes of *Exploring Heavenly Places*

59. Leviticus 18:1-30

60. Genesis 3:15

61. Genesis 10:1-32

62. Acts 2:1-41

63. Genesis 12:4-9

64. Genesis 12:11-15

65. Genesis 3:15

66. Genesis 12:17-19, 13:1-2

67. Genesis 14:1-2

68. Genesis 14:5

69. Biblical Training; http://www.biblicaltraining.org/library/zuzim

Chapter 8

70. Ezekiel 16:48-50

71. Genesis 13:12

72. Genesis 19:15-25

73. Genesis 19:30-33

74. Genesis 19:34-35

75. Wikipedia, The Free Encyclopedia; http://en.wikipedia.org/wiki/Moloch

76. Micah 6:7

77. Wikipedia, The Free Encyclopedia; http://en.wikipedia.org/wiki/Baal

78. Jeremiah 19:4-5, 32:35

79. Deuteronomy 32:8

80. Leviticus 18:1-30

81. Follow the Rabbi; http://followtherabbi.com/guide/detail/fertility-cults-of-canaan

82. Yahoo! Answers; https://answers.yahoo.com/question/index?qid=20100927181835AAZ8I5O

83. An in-depth discussion of gates and doors will be included in a succeeding volume of Exploring Heavenly Places

84. Psalm 24:6-8; Isaiah 45:1-3

85. Genesis 22:15-17, 24:60, 28:10-17

86. Matthew 16:13-19

87. Deuteronomy 4:43, Joshua 21:27

88. Genesis 14:5; Deuteronomy 3:13; Joshua 12:4, 13:12

89. 2 Samuel 5:20-22

90. http://www.abarim-publications.com/Meaning/Rephaim.html#.VCYGjlZycTs

Chapter 9

91. Leviticus 18:21, 20:2-5

92. 1 Kings 11:1-8, 12:31; 2 Kings 23:10

93. Genesis 10:6

94. Creation Ministries International; http://creation.com/egyptian-history-and-the-biblical-record-a-perfect-match

95. Deuteronomy 32:8

96. Answers From the Book; http://answersfromthebook.org/2011/02/28/the-living-god-vs-the-gods-of-egypt/

97. Psalm 106:19-23

98. Acts 6:8

99. Acts 7:1-53

100. Deuteronomy 4:19

101. Psalm 106:19-39

102. Numbers 13:27-33

103. Deuteronomy 9:1-3

104. Wikipedia, The Free Encyclopedia;http://en.wikipedia.org/wiki/ Death_of_Osama_bin_Laden

105. Deuteronomy 9:4-6

106. Wikipedia, The Free Encyclopedia; http://en.wikipedia.org/wiki/ Ru dolf_Wanderone

107. Joshua 5:13-15

108. Ask; http://www.ask.com/question/meaning-of-jericho

109. Ancient Days; http://davelivingston.com/mooncity.htm

110. Joshua 6:15, 12-20

111. Joshua 6:21-23

112. Joshua 7:2-4

113. Deuteronomy 27-28

114. Galatians 6:2

115. Genesis 10:9-10

116. Wikipedia, The Free Encyclopedia; http://en.wikipedia.org/wiki/Baby lon

117. Genesis 11:28, 31

118. Easton, M. G., *Easton's Bible Dictionary*

119. Ancient Mesopotamian Gods and Goddesses; http://oracc.museum. upenn.edu/amgg/listofdeities/nannasuen/index.html

120. Truth Magazine; http://www.truthmagazine.com/archives/volume20/ GOT020218.html

121. Deuteronomy 4:19

122. Joshua 6:18, 7:1

Chapter 10

123. 1 Samuel 17:1-11, 23

124. Genesis 6:1-4

125. http://www.abarim-publications.com/Meaning/Goliath.html#.VCiOH ktycTs

126. Sid Roth's It's Supernatural; http://sidroth.org/articles/ real-meaning-jerusalem-lane

127. Ibid.

128. Matthew 16:18

129. liftjesuscross; http://liftjesuscross.com/2012/02/05/golgotha-the-place-of-the-skull/

130. Webster's Online Dictionary; http://www.webster-dictionary.org /definition/fractal

131. Fractal Foundation; http://fractalfoundation.org/resources/what-are-fractals/

132. 1 Kings 11:7

133. 2 Kings 18:10-12; Jeremiah 25:9-12

134. Jeremiah 3:6-15

135. 2 Samuel 11:1-5

136. 1 Kings 11:1-11

137. 1 Kings 11:43

138. 1 Kings 12:20

139. 1 Kings 12:26-28

140. 1 Kings 12:29-31

141. gotQuestions?org; http://www.gotquestions.org/who-Baal.html

142. Jeremiah 32:35

143. Bibloscope; http://bibloscope.com/content/kaleidoscopic-views/names-baal

144. 1 Kings 16:31

145. Ezekiel 28:11-13

146. 1 Kings 16:33, 17:1

147. Wikipedia, The Free Encyclopedia; http://en.wikipedia.org/wiki/Jezebel

148. 1 Kings 18:13-14

149. 1 Kings 18:21-40

150. 1 Kings 18:31-32, 38-39

151. 1 Kings 18:41-45; Luke 4:25

152. Blogspot; http://gregboyd.blogspot.com/2008/06/boyd-and- heiser-dialogue-on-nephilim.html

153. Deuteronomy 32:7-8

154. Leviticus 18:24-28

Chapter 11

155. Isaiah 14:9

156. Abarim Publications; http://www.abarim-publications.com /Meaning/ Rephaim.html#.VCiVK0tycTs

157. Job 26:5; Isaiah 14:9; Psalm 88:10

158. Isaiah 14:9-11

159. Wikipedia, The Free Encyclopedia; http://en.wikipedia.org/wiki/Sheol

160. http://www.scribd.com/doc/68024391/Serpent-Seed-Dr-Michael-S-Heiser p.6

161. Ibid., p 7

Chapter 12

162. Romans 8:19

163. Genesis 3:7-10

164. Strong's Concordance 5206; http://www.lexiconcordance.com/greek/5206.html

165. Louw, J.P., Nida, Eugene Albert, (1998) *Greek-English Lexicon of the New Testament: Based on Semantic Domains.* New York, NY: United Bible Societies.

166. John 1:12

167. Luke 3:38

168. Ephesians 1:3; 2:6

169. Stott, John R., (1994) *Romans, God's Good News for the World* (238). Leicester, England; Downers Grove, IL: InterVarsity Press.

170. Bible StudyTools; http://www.biblestudytools.com/lexicons/greek/nas/

171. *http://www.sonstoglory.com/spiritualadoption.htm*

172. Ibid.

173. Ibid.

174. Matthew 3:16-17

175. Ephesians 1:3-6

Chapter 13

176. Wikipedia, The Free Encyclopedia; http://en.wikipedia.org/wiki/Hurricane_Iselle_(2014)

177. Baby Name Facts; http://www.babynamefacts.com/babynames/summary.php?name=iselle#.VCievEtycTs

178. Wikipedia, The Free Encyclopedia; http://en.wikipedia.org/wiki/Aysel

179. Our Baby Namer; http://www.ourbabynamer.com/meaning-of-Julio.

180. Johnny Enlow; http://rainbowgod.com/johnny-elizabeth-enlow/

181. 1 Kings 17:17-22

182. 1 Kings 18:20-40).

183. Isaiah 40:3-5, 57:14, 62:10

184. Malachi 4:5-6

185. Luke 1:17

Chapter 14

186. Ephesians 4:11-13

187. Greek Word Studies; http://greekwordstudies.blogspot.com/2007/04/equip.html

188. Greek Word Studies; http://greekwordstudies.blogspot.com/2007/04/equip.html

189. Matthew 28:18-20

190. Oxford Dictionaries; http://www.oxforddictionaries.com/us/definition/ american_english/orphan

191. Wikipedia, The Free Dictionary; http://en.wikipedia.org/wiki/Orphan

192. Matthew 3:17

193. Strong's Concordance 2106; http://www.lexiconcordance.com / greek/2106.html

194. Psalm 16:11

195. Romans 8:15

196. Ephesians 1:3

197. Hebrews 5:14; 1 Corinthians 1:17-18

198. Derek Prince; http://www.google.com/url?sa=t&rct=j&q=&esrc=s&source=web&cd=1&ved=0CCAQFjAA&url=http%3A%2F%2Fwww.derekprince.org%2FPublisher%2FFile.aspx%3Fid%3D1000021528&ei=2aMoVPa7BofaoATCsoKYCA&usg=AFQjCNGk5Uz6w9DIfAUCvMNymWFyKC5-uA&sig2=4DWhsiMXgwiuaCnoYffbOw&bvm=bv.76247554,d.cGU

199. Garr, John D., (2003). *Family Sanctuary: Restoring The Biblically Hebraic Home* (39-43, 50-55). Golden Key Press.

200. Ezekiel 5:1-17; Hosea 1:1-11

Chapter 15

201. Genesis 14:18–20

202. It is interesting that there are nine kings mentioned and in Hebrews Melchizedek is mentioned nine times.

203. Wikipedia, The Free Encyclopedia; http://en.wikipedia.org/wiki/Amra phel

204. Genesis 10:9. In Genesis 6:4 the same word for mighty, *geber,* is used to describe the Nephilim, the children of the fallen sons of God.

205. See previous chapters about the moon god.

206. Wikipedia, The Free Encyclopedia; http://en.wikipedia.org/wiki/Arioch

207. Elwell, W. A., & Comfort, P. W. (2001). In *Tyndale Bible Dictionary.* Wheaton, IL: Tyndale House Publishers.

208. Wikipedia, The Free Encyclopedia; http://en.wikipedia.org/wiki/Tidal_ (Bible)

209. Strong, J. (2001). *Enhanced Strong's Lexicon.* Bellingham, WA: Logos Bible Software.

210. Easton, M. G. (1893). In *Easton's Bible dictionary.* New York: Harper & Brothers.

211. Myers, A. C. (1987). *The Eerdmans Bible dictionary* (943). Grand Rapids, MI: Eerdmans

212. Strong, J. (2001). *Enhanced Strong's Lexicon.* Bellingham, WA: Logos Bible Software.

213. Strong, J. (2001). *Enhanced Strong's Lexicon.* Bellingham, WA: Logos Bible Software.

214. Genesis 14:4

215. Harris, R. L., Archer, G. L., Jr., & Waltke, B. K. (Eds.). (1999). *Theologi cal Wordbook of the Old Testament.* Chicago: Moody Press.

216. See previous chapters about the tie between Ashtoreth and Baal and the fallen sons of God.

217. Strong, J. (2001). *Enhanced Strong's Lexicon.* Bellingham, WA: Logos Bible Software.

218. Strong, J. (2001). *Enhanced Strong's Lexicon.* Bellingham, WA: Logos Bible Software.

219. Strong, J. (2001). *Enhanced Strong's Lexicon.* Bellingham, WA: Logos Bible Software.

220. Salem means peace. Often we are taught that Melchizedek was the king

of a place called Salem, which eventually became Jerusalem. I believe the phrase should be translated "King of Peace."

221. Psalm 110: 1-2,4

222. John 8:56

Chapter 16

223. Boyd, Gregory. (1997). *God at War* (282). Leicester, England; Downers Grove, IL: InterVarsity Press.

Chapter 20

224. Key Scriptures for the prayer are: Job 38:33; Psalm 24, 110:2; Proverbs 8; Isaiah 28; Jeremiah 2:13; Daniel 7, 9:4-6, 11; Colossians 2: 13, 14; Revelation 11:15-17, 12:10-12

Appendix

225. Signs & Wonders Studio/Creation Restorations http://www.creationrestorations.com/index.html jana@creationrestorations.com. Email: jana@creationrestorations.com>

226. Larry & Jacqueline Pearson, Lion Sword Communications pearsons@lionsword.net and www.lionsword.ca

227. Key.bearer@hotmail.com

228. Dawn@newreflectionministries.org

Printed in Great Britain
by Amazon

80494702R00078